God's Word

---

for a

Complex World:

Discovering how
the Bible speaks today

God's Word

---

for a

Complex World:

Discovering how
the Bible speaks today

Andrew Kirk

Marshall Pickering

Marshall Morgan and Scott
Marshall Pickering
3 Beggarwood Lane, Basingstoke, Hants RG23 7LP, UK

Copyright © 1987 J. Andrew Kirk
First published in 1987 by Marshall Morgan and Scott Publications
Ltd
Part of the Marshall Pickering Holdings Group
A subsidiary of the Zondervan Corporation

British Library CIP Data
Kirk, Andrew
God's Word for a Complex World.
1. Christian life – 1960--
I. Title
248.4 BV4501.2

ISBN 0–551–01437–7

Phototypeset in Linotron Ehrhardt 11 on 12pt by
Input Typesetting Ltd, London SW19 8DR
Printed in Great Britain by Guernsey Press Ltd, Guernsey C.I.

Contents

Preface

Questions about exactly *how* to relate the Bible to modern life have been with me for a long time. Only the seriousness and complexity of the task have kept me from writing before now.

I had hoped that someone else, more capable than myself, would have already tackled the subject and produced a book. If one does exist, I am unaware of it. Therefore, I have felt compelled, reluctantly, to put pen to paper myself.

Ordinary Christian people I have met in London, elsewhere in Britain and overseas have, perhaps unconsciously, urged me on by the questions they have asked. They are at the sharp end of Christian witness and discipleship, often in situations of indifference or hostility to Christian belief and values. As a result, many of them are calling for help in the task of reflecting, from a biblical point of view, on the world they live in. I am afraid the present book is only a modest contribution. Perhaps it will stimulate others to do a better job.

I am grateful, as always, to many friends with whom, over the years, I have discussed the issues about which I am writing. In particular I would single out colleagues in the London Institute for Contemporary Christianity – Martyn Eden, Ernest Lucas, Roy McCoughry and John Stott – who have given precious time to delve into the text. Their comments have been invaluable. Needless to say, they are not accomplices to my errors.

Janet Barker, in a rash moment of extreme generosity, agreed to type the manuscript from my handwriting. I owe her, too, a great debt of gratitude. She worked a series of miracles in creating an amazingly clean manuscript.

All biblical quotations are from the New International Version, unless otherwise stated.

Andrew Kirk, London, October 1986

To Daniel, Alasdair and Nicola:
That they may believe and
live by God's Word
all their days

Introduction

1 The point of the exercise

The task I have set myself is far from easy. No book has ever been more minutely studied than the Bible. People who claim that in its pages the way of salvation and right living is spelt out for all races feel passionately about the results of the study. The human tendency to disagree sharply on most issues under the sun has affected the Bible's interpretation. Differences of opinion have been so acute that some people conclude that contrasting understandings of the message are not only probable but even desirable.

In the midst of this controversy about the original meaning of the words and their contemporary relevance, one embarks on a study of the Bible's application with much trepidation. Two particular reasons motivate me. First, although a neutral approach to interpretation is impossible, I cannot accept that one's understanding of the message is purely a matter of individual taste. On the contrary, by applying certain methods, students of the Bible should be able to move towards a common mind. Many of the differences are due to an insistence on only one approach. If we listen to and consider what other people have discovered in the text, a much greater degree of consensus is possible. The question is, how to discover the appropriate methods and enable real listening to take place.

Secondly, I am sure that there is an urgent need for a

sensitive, discerning and precise application of the Bible's message to numerous aspects of modern human life. This conviction springs from the belief that the Bible contains the only information which can permanently reverse the natural tendency of all human beings to destroy relationships based on mutual respect and trust. In other words, only by discovering a reliable way of bringing the biblical message to bear on modern life can people recapture hope.

This belief gives to the task of interpretation a sense of mission which cannot be evaded. The gravity of the task should call forth a strong desire to learn the right way of doing things. To allow the Bible to speak God's Word in the contemporary world demands the patient assimilation of certain skills whose possession cannot be taken for granted.

All who are committed to the Bible's central figure, the Father of Jesus Christ, need to become adept in 'rightly handling the word of truth'. Paul writing to Timothy (2 Tim 2:15) uses the metaphor of the craftsman. Handling this word of truth is not a mechanical operation which can be learnt simply by applying a set of techniques. It involves the mastery of skills which will help to relate the text to contemporary social and personal existence.

The model, then, for this study of biblical interpretation is that of the apprentice. In the course of training the apprentice will be given the right tools to use, be shown how to use them, become proficient by actually using them and finally be able to help others develop the same expertise. The model is a marvellous example of what the process of learning is all about. Understanding the Bible is also a learning process in which the reader is continually stimulated to inquire and investigate. The basic motive has to be a curiosity to know how the Bible helps us to discover God's will for us today.

I hope to be able to display something of the unique power of the biblical message to speak an appropriate and penetrating word to our confused and distraught world. I believe that the message demands a response and only those, therefore, prepared to agree with its diagnosis and prescription for a fully human life can benefit from its teaching. This book is about trying to help such people integrate more fully their commitment to Jesus Christ with the life of the world around them.

Studying the Bible is not principally an academic exercise. The main intention is not to possess accurate knowledge, though that is important; rather it is to express how, by progressing in faithfulness to the Lord over all lords, one may enjoy real freedom and discover a lasting purpose in life.

Whatever the time-scale and however God shapes the future, Jesus' disciples are called to be faithful to the way God has revealed himself in his plan of salvation, in his laws and in his constant activity to make new life in Jesus concrete in human situations. This revelation has been given in a wholly unique, because pure and comprehensive, form in the pages of the Old and New Testament. It is only this text, among all the many claims to spiritual and moral enlightenment in our pluralistic world, which comes with the binding authority of the Creator of all things.

Followers of Jesus Christ are called to be responsible servants, faithful over a little, practising a stewardship of whatever gifts God may have given them, not attempting to emulate those gifts which the Father may have given to others among his children. I trust that this book will enable us to exercise our talents with more skill, so that the knowledge of God and the fragrance of life in Jesus may extend to more people and to their social situations.

Disciples of Jesus, by learning how to apply the transforming force of God's good news to the intricacies of life, can challenge and subvert all cultures which have substituted human ambitions and gratifications for the worship of God and the service of people in need. In particular the time has come for them to press for changes in certain aspects of Western secular civilisation: the cult of individual attainment, intellectual snobbery, cultural arrogance and an economically and politically aggressive stance towards vulnerable and defenceless peoples across the globe.

The message of the Bible continues to be the most

powerful weapon that anyone can possess, both to destroy attitudes and institutions which counter God's demands and to create in their place something beautiful and wholesome for him.

2 Difficulties in the way

The vision of what we want to achieve may be clear. Obstacles, however, may prevent us from reaching our goals. Taking a good look at them and measuring their difficulties, as a horserider does to fences before a round of jumps, may help us to clear them. In the following three areas there are questions which make the task of interpretation problematical.

(a) The Bible under fire

(i) A book from long ago A cluster of problems exist for those who want to claim that the Bible speaks the truth. It is an ancient text; parts go back more than 3,000 years and all of it was written 1,900 years ago or more. It deals with situations, customs and beliefs which are bound to seem remote to a culture built on a belief in progress and the superiority of the latest ideas. How can one possibly expect a group of writings from so distant a past to say anything relevant to our vastly different situation? We might read it as an interesting account of the history and religious convictions of a small tribe from the Fertile Crescent. There seems, however, so little in it which actually touches the complexities of our way of life and so much in our world which is not even hinted at in the text.

Even if one were able to make some direct connections between two such foreign worlds, why should the Bible be granted any privileged status? We are accustomed today to live in a society which prides itself on its religious tolerance. The result of such tolerance and of the banishment of religious commitment to the area of private, subjective and individual feeling is that almost anything goes in religion. The availability of many different forms of religion, offering the consumer a wide range of choices, accords well with the type of life we practise.

(ii) Truth to tell Perhaps the hardest problem which modern people face when looking at the Bible is its frequent claim to state the truth about human life: 'teach me your way, O Lord, and I will walk in your truth' (Ps 86:11); 'Jesus answered . . . for this reason I was born, and for this I came into the world, to testify to the truth' (Jn 18:37); 'assuming you were taught in him, in accordance with the truth that is in Jesus' (Eph 4:21).

There can be no doubt about the specific nature of the claim. However, it sounds out of place today, a relic from the past, no longer acceptable to a generation taught to think critically. For a number of reasons the idea of truth as a universally valid and permanent set of statements about the nature and meaning of life and death seems incredible.

First, it is claimed that real knowledge in a scientific world can only be discovered by research, experiment and experience. Knowledge which comes by any other channel, communicated somehow from another realm of existence, is speculative and dubious. In principle such knowledge can be neither verified nor proved false. Moreover, science prefers to speak of statements being provisional, not immutable. The idea that we are dependent on another means of understanding our world than that of rational, logical investigation sticks in the throat. To many it is simply unacceptable.

Secondly, because we human beings live in a stream of changing historical events, any absolute truth, if it does exist, can only be known at the end of the process. Truth seems to be always beyond the horizon. It seems, therefore, quite absurd to claim that truth can be based on a number of historical incidents which took place long ago. Furthermore, it is of the essence of historical evidence that it may be unreliable. At the least, our attempt to get at the real facts is an uncertain process.

Thirdly, as a result of our modern preoccupation with what works, claims to truth have to be tested by the role they play. Convictions about life, death, human relationships and right and wrong are true in so far as they appear to help people cope better with their problems. Like almost everything else we relate to, truth is considered a commodity to be possessed and moulded to serve our ends. We find it hard to tolerate a concept of truth which makes demands on us, irrespective of our convenience, and a reality which shapes us, rather than being fashioned by us.

(iii) What about the scholars? If these arguments do not seem to destroy any residual confidence we may have in the ability of the Bible to give us facts about life we could not find elsewhere, there is the widely acclaimed belief that a critical, scholarly approach to the Bible has made acceptance of many historical facts as they are presented in it well-nigh impossible.

Biblical scholars have reckoned to uncover a whole host of oral traditions and written scripts behind the finished text as we have received it. They believe that most books of the Bible have been formed over a period of time by weaving together a number of strands. Quite often these different traditions express diverse, if not contradictory, beliefs. Moreover, in the course of time much of the story-telling has become embellished, often with apologetic motives, so that as statements of anything close to what really happened the biblical books are untrustworthy.

The general consequence of critical scholarship is to undermine confidence in the authority of the Bible. It is usually accepted in those circles that the Bible must be approached as if it were any other text from the ancient Near East. It cannot be exempted from the canons of normal, critical scrutiny.

(iv) Reasons for accepting the Bible's authority I do not intend to respond at this stage to the objections discussed above. I will pick them up gradually in the course of the book. Here, I want to state what I think are the main reasons for conceding that the Bible has to be listened to with an attention which no other writing merits. There are four interlocking arguments.

First, intellectual honesty demands that we should

consider carefully what the Bible claims to be. We have already noted in passing that it makes unrivalled and audacious affirmations about the absolute and final truth of its message. Truth, by its very nature, makes claims upon our consciences and wills. It demands a response of some kind. This may be 'Yes' or 'No'.

Because of the far-reaching nature of the claims in this case, an attempt to be non-committal is as good as refusing to say 'Yes'. No-one can remain on some neutral ground, pretending to possess a disinterested vantage-point as they listen to the text saying, for example, 'you shall love the Lord your God (with all you have) and your neighbour as yourself' or 'the wages of (your) sin is death, but God's gift (to you) is eternal life in Christ Jesus our Lord'. Such direct commands and statements demand either acceptance or repudiation. Both courses of action bring with them considerable consequences.

Secondly, the message itself presents us with a wholly unique combination of teaching. Though parts of the Bible have parallels in other religions and philosophies from Egypt, Babylon and Greece, and though other religious traditions possess similar beliefs at certain points, the differences are far more marked. Indeed, so divergent is the biblical teaching about creation, the cause and effects of sin and God's plan of salvation from anything other religions proclaim, that many students of comparative faiths conclude that the message of the Bible is a continual protest against religion. By this they mean that at every major point the Bible contradicts the natural religious inclinations of human beings: for example, that salvation is dependent on the way we live, that we need human mediators to help us reach God, that prayer is about getting God on our side, that systems of belief have the function of promoting order and stability in society. There is a sense, then, in which the Bible's message carries its own internal authority, as it confronts human beings with a denial of their religiosity. As Paul of Tarsus once said, 'by setting forth the truth plainly we commend ourselves to every man's conscience in the sight of God' (2 Cor 4:2).

Thirdly, the impact of the Bible upon the life of individuals, cultures and civilisations has been massive. We could not of course deny, even if we wanted to, that many who claim to be following biblical teaching have brought suffering and humiliation to thousands of people. What has sometimes been done in the name of Jesus Christ almost defies imagination: the Crusades, the Inquisition, the wholesale destruction of cultures, apartheid and so on. Nevertheless, each of these and many more are clearly perversions of the total biblical revelation of God. They are examples of the way in which biblical faith can be distorted and converted into a religion which is then used to promote sectional interests.

On the other side, people responding rightly to the Bible have struggled against the 'divine' right of certain human institutions to possess for all time an unchallengeable power and authority, been pioneers in scientific research, campaigned for the abolition of slavery, child labour and the exploitation of workers, championed prison reform and been in the forefront of campaigns to eradicate scourges like leprosy, illiteracy and the caste system. And this list has only begun. The Bible's authority is disclosed through the fruits of change it produces when people take its whole message seriously.

Finally, the Bible's claims can be compared with all rival ones. Contrary to a generally accepted modern belief, there can be no real freedom from authority. Human beings do not live in a moral and spiritual limbo. If the old gods are declared illusions and crutches and are swept out of the front door, new demons will enter by the back window. It is an observable fact of human life that we need stable points of reference to specify how we should behave. These may be traditions from the past, cultural norms in the present, rational discourse, obligations to the family, submission to the State, ideologies and even fashionable but transitory opinions.

The problem with each one of these is that it is based on a partial and therefore inadequate view of what it means to be human. Human nature is constituted in such a way that either we submit ourselves to the true and living God or we allow ourselves to be taken over by some substitute. Life cannot be lived on the basis of countless open options. To believe we are free from the binding claims of some authority or other is a dangerous illusion.

So far these arguments about authority are somewhat theoretical. To acknowledge that the Bible is an authority which lays claims upon us and the societies in which we live is not made as a formal declaration or as a ritual observation. It is taken as a stance of faith which is tested by action.

The Bible's authority in the life of an individual or a community is measured in practice. Moreover, the kind of authority we allow to the biblical text can only be judged finally by the way we handle it. A confessional statement about the authority of the Bible may give people a clue as to what Christian tradition we come from, but it will not necessarily guarantee that at all times we use a correct method of interpretation. Such a conviction will shape the way we read the text and apply it – it will not automatically preserve us from insensitive and inappropriate conclusions.

The Bible's authority is transmitted through its message. What we make of the message will demonstrate how we have been conducting our interpretation. This in turn will reveal how we perceive its authority. God's truth is never just a statement of the way things are, it is always a call to action. The Bible's authority is not, therefore, a matter of intellectual assent, but of practice: 'Now that you know these things, you will be blessed if you do them' (John 13:17).

(b) The complexity of modern day reality

Only a fool would claim that he fully understands the trends in contemporary science, art, politics, ethical behaviour, communications and economic life. Many times, when one begins to sense that events are falling into straightforward patterns, a new discovery, fact or interpretation comes along to upset calculations.

A right judgement about the overall structure of modern life and of its various interlinking parts is only possible from a perspective which has answers to the ultimate questions of existence: birth and death, sickness and suffering, success and failure, the meaning of life, the various stages of human development and how to handle human differences (gender, race, economic position, social standing). Though glib, simplistic responses to these profound realities should be resisted, the Bible as a record of God's communication does offer a totally adequate perspective from which to make sense of all that surrounds us.

From this perspective, little by little, always open to correction and new insights, a student of the Bible can understand such things as *the meaning of historical processes* (for example, the student rebellion of the 1960s or the revitalisation of the peace movement in the 1980s), *motives for behaviour* (e.g. why people follow trends in fashion), and *the reasons for stances and actions* (e.g. why, in general, human beings respond more readily to the call to alleviate the eye-catching symptoms of hunger than to eliminating its causes)

Then, also, the person who reads the Bible carefully can discover how to offer purpose, direction and meaningful change to individual human life and its collective enterprises. He or she will find that both these major tasks constitute a vocation for life. They are part of the responsibility of anyone who desires above all else to serve God and neighbour.

(c) The confusion of Christian responses

It would be wholly naive to pretend that all those who seek to relate the Bible to contemporary issues are of a common mind. There is an unfortunate babble of opinions among Christians today. None of us are free from blame in contributing to the confusion. There are a number of contributing factors: widely differing views about the trustworthiness of the Bible; the adoption of doctrines and ideologies which the text is allowed to support and justify but not criticise; distortions produced by the felt need to defend our customs, way of life or national pride; obsessions with single issues, however important (like racial or sexual discrimination, sexual ethics, family life, the state of the poor, peace and violence, personal experiences); the defence of denominational beliefs and traditions (such as ordination, the way baptism is administered, discipline, the appointment of leaders, doctrines of the Church).

The task of understanding and applying the Bible has to take into consideration all these reasons for disagreement. Part of the task is to discover how students of the Bible can increasingly agree, in spite of the forces which pull them apart. What are the ways of overcoming these circumstances, often accidental, which contribute to the rifts and controversies among us? What steps can we take to move slowly together as we consider our responsibility to share the gospel of Jesus Christ, be involved in the struggle to right wrong and bring love and justice into human relationships?

3 The course of action

The broad subject matter of this book is, to use a term of the trade, hermeneutics. By this I mean two closely related tasks: first, the discovery and use of principles to guide the application of the biblical message to every day life; secondly, an analysis of what goes on in our world in the light of the Bible. The two projects are complementary. They work in tandem from both ends of a bridge. They are both indispensable.

A number of books have already been written on the subject of the general rules of interpretation (see the suggestions for further reading at the end). My concern will not, therefore, be to repeat what others have done with great competence before me. I will, however, touch on them in so far as is necessary to deal adequately with the whole subject of the book. My particular interest is how we use the Bible to get to grips with the serious questions of our history.

It seems to me that if the Bible is to disclose its significance to us where we are, at least four different tasks have to be undertaken. They are isolated here in order to give a clearer idea of a process. In practice they will not be so neatly distinguished. First, as a method of concentrating on specific texts, there is *exegesis*. This is an inductive approach to interpretation. Its aim is to discover what the original writer meant to communicate by the words and phrases he used. Exegesis is the task of laying bare the original sense of a passage. Close attention has to be given to the use of language and to the historical context from which the writing comes.

Secondly, there is *exposition*. Here an attempt is made to apply the author's original concerns to the situation of contemporary listeners. Commentaries on books of the Bible often attempt this, as does preaching. Naturally, one of the crucial questions to be faced in the task of exposition concerns the affinity between the situation of the first recipients of the message and ours today. A vital part of the task, then, is to decide what it is about human life, despite changes in external circumstances, which remains constant through the ages.

Thirdly, there is *elucidation*. This is the work of formulating questions from our context to the text of the Bible. If the biblical message, as God's Word to his special creatures, is 'a lamp to [our] feet and a light for [our] path' (Ps 119:105), what particular matters do we want it to illuminate? This part of the process of discovering how the Bible speaks today needs to pay special attention to discovering the nature of the problems we face. We begin, then, by clarifying the situation in which we live and the challenge it poses to 'the truth which is in Jesus'.

Fourthly, there is *extraction*. This a deductive approach to interpretation, for it is concerned to discover from the text and from contemporary life principles which will guide action in those aspects of our experience not directly addressed by the text. Because of scientific advance, the recent bringing together of different cultures through travel, migration and mass communication and the development of beliefs, ideas and institutions, the Bible inevitably is silent about a number of matters which directly preoccupy us two or three thousand years later. Nevertheless, the Bible is concerned about the whole of human life. How, then, may we extract material that would be relevant to particularly modern issues like the use of nuclear energy and test-tube babies?

In the course of the book I hope to give some guidance on how each one of these tasks can be undertaken, and how each relates to the others. I will concentrate, however, on the last two, because, as far as I know, they are rarely touched upon in studies of Biblical interpretation.

Conclusion

In order to earth the whole process I want to try to relate the whole exercise to specific questions of a broadly political nature.[1] This is obviously intended to be of service specifically to those engaged in, or who think seriously about, political life at different levels. But, by analogy, the method should be easily adaptable to any aspect of life, so that a person who wants to learn how to use the Bible and make sense of it has a model already available. I realise there are particular dangers in wanting to focus on politics as the concrete example of the method we want to explore. No-one can pretend to be neutral or disinterested about political matters. All of us have certain convictions, which find their support more in one political philosophy, party or programme than another. Politics is undoubtedly an emotive and divisive field for discussion. There is the probability that one's own political persuasions will influence to some extent the way one handles biblical interpretation. I am at least aware of the hazards and pitfalls.

On the other side, I would argue that the very nature of the hermeneutical task demands that we enter into the heart of the real world, which is full of controversy and disagreement. Though it is important not to invest politics with more weight and substance than it merits, the reality touches all of us in most areas of our lives. We cannot retreat from the political reality which surrounds us into a private world unaffected by the need to balance different interests and needs within 'the community'. Moreover, many of Jesus Christ's disciples are wanting to know more about how they may influence political life, so that policies and decisions approximate more to God's will on earth as in heaven.

The Bible relates a story of a people who were, of necessity, deeply immersed in activities of a definitely political nature, or which had profound political implications. It seems to me, therefore, that the risk of bringing together the Bible and politics is worth taking. No doubt, critics will point out my mistakes. As a result, the process of understanding and applying the Bible will be refined, so that all of us committed to the faith of Jesus Christ may be more competent interpreters and more active in his service.

Notes

1   However, the intention of the book is *not* to explore a biblical view of politics. It should *not*, therefore, be read in this light. The purpose is to look at how to use the Bible in deciding what to believe and how to act in the modern world. Politics is simply one instance, albeit important, of this process. Other examples (e.g. war and peace, the relationship between men and women in the home, society and the Church, marriage and divorce, revolution and development) could equally well have been chosen.

There will be a natural tendency among readers of this book to expect specific conclusions to be drawn about contemporary political life in the light of the Bible. Again, this is *not* my intention. Rather, I am trying to illustrate a process of interpretation and application. Hence, I would not give the answers if I had them (which I don't), for this would deprive the readers of the opportunity of using the methods for themselves and drawing their own conclusions. In a word, the book is about *how*, not *what*.

I

Approaching With The Right Outlook

This book is written with the conviction that the Bible presents a unique perspective on our human life, and also that ordinary people, without specialist knowledge, can adequately discover its meaning for their situation.

However, except in special and rare circumstances, the meaning does not come to us like a flash. Some people may be granted immediate access to God's will which does not pass through the normal channels of thought, discussion and reflection. Such an experience is an exception to the way God usually expects us to understand what he is saying.

As we live in a climate of opinion today where exaggerated claims to personal experience abound, we should not accept every revelation just because it is said to come from God. We should test the claims, in order to distinguish what is truly of God from what is a matter of personal insight or opinion. The ability to discern true belief and practice from false is a key mark of spiritual maturity in the Christian life – 'Do not despise inspired messages. Put all things to the test: keep what is good and avoid every kind of evil' (1 Thess 5:20–22, TEV).

For most people, uncovering and applying the meaning of the message and testing other people's views will require us to apply methods which help us to discover what is right. No-one has access to an infallible interpretation, however reassuring it might be to think one does. Nevertheless, God's revelation is not a complicated puzzle which only those with a high IQ can work at. Far from it. He reveals himself truly to anyone prepared to listen honestly and openly. To hear we need to consider a few important principles. The following seem to me the most crucial.

1 Acceptance of the Bible's nature and purpose

The first principle of interpretation is to understand the Bible from its own point of view. What does it say about itself? What is its nature? How did it come to be written? Why does it exist at all?

Briefly we might describe the Bible as both a record of God's actions in the world and an explanation of those actions. Such a definition summarises the conviction of Amos: 'the Sovereign Lord never does anything without revealing his plan to his servants, the prophets' (Amos 3:7).

The Bible tells us about three fundamental realities: God, human life and the physical world. It explains how each is meant to relate to the others and why, in the case of humans, relationships have broken down. These three reference points provide a framework in which we can make sense of all the details of our existence.

The Bible's message is not simply a set of timeless truths. It is God's *Word*, which has been spoken in specific historical situations and for special reasons. God has also given us his *Spirit* to re-apply the Word to our situations. As Jesus said to important religious leaders of his day, we will believe and act wrongly, unless we know both the Scriptures and the power of God (Mk 12:24).

The purpose for which the Bible was written is summed up by Paul in a letter to Timothy (2 Tim 3:15–17). It shows, first, how we may be rescued from the mess we make both of our own lives and of the natural world around us and, secondly, how we may fulfil God's perfect and just demands.

Accepting the nature and purpose of the Bible is a first step in understanding it. Together they help us appreciate what we may expect to find there. They also indicate ways in which we should relate the text to our situation. By an inductive process, we find out what the Bible says on a topic (e.g. justice). By a deductive process we seek to draw appropriate conclusions concerning such matters as justice in industrial relations and in the matter of civil liberties.

2 A willingness to listen

Obviously we will not learn anything from the Bible if we have already made up our mind what we want to hear. Nevertheless, it is hard for most of us to read and study the text with a mind sufficiently open to have our cherished notions challenged if need be. We already come with a whole suitcase full of opinions and ideas imbibed from our family, society, peer-group, religious tradition, or by reaction to any or all of these. Because our own identity is often bound up with our convictions, we may feel deeply threatened by the idea that they could easily be questioned by the text.

The Bible also has plenty of convictions of its own. It makes numerous claims and demands which cut right across how we perceive life. Its statements about God, about the cause of and remedy for evil, and about moral matters may well conflict with strongly-held beliefs which motivate and direct our response to the world as we see it. There is a real possibility that the Bible will cut right across what we think is reasonable. For example, the apostle Paul is only echoing a general sentiment of the Bible when he says that 'God has shown that this world's wisdom is foolishness!' (1 Cor 1:20). In other words, many of the conclusions people come to on the basis of their own experience and thinking are false when compared with the Bible's view.

Moreover, we are often exhorted to specific action. Anyone reading the story of Jesus' life knows that he begins his public ministry by calling people in general to turn from their past way of life, to believe the Good News that through him a new kind of existence is possible and to follow him. The commands are so direct that anyone hearing them has to say either 'Yes' or 'No'. In the circumstances, attempting to sit on the fence means, 'I don't want to change'.

If we are not ready to face the challenge of believing and acting, we are forced to evade the implications of what is being said. We may respond bluntly, 'I cannot accept that anyone has the right to interfere with my life in this way,' or, 'I don't believe this story can be taken seriously any more.' We may seek to avoid the call to change by more sophisticated strategies: we may be tempted, for example, to say either that the history of Jesus is unreliable because the gospel writers were biased, or that there are many other equally acceptable ways of serving God and other people.

Whatever reason is given, a person attempting to take evasive action must have a sufficiently good reason for denying the claims of the Bible upon his or her life. We can only say its description of God and human life is wrong if we have an alternative source of truth by which to measure it. Mere opinion, when not verified either by indisputable fact or convincing argument, is mere prejudice. An alternative source of truth can only come from outside our own minds. In the nature of the case the source of truth is independent of our thinking and experience though grasped by them. The source may be another religious tradition or a philosophy which denies validity to any religious experience, like humanist thinking and Marxist ideology. It is crucial to realise that we cannot adopt a neutral position, free of prior intellectual and moral commitment, from which objectively to measure the truth, or error, of the Bible's message. We cannot stand outside ourselves or our corner of the world.

The Bible itself shows why neutrality is impossible: human beings cannot live in a vacuum of unbelief. Thinking and acting presuppose a set of beliefs that are more or less coherent and true to life. One person's belief is another person's unbelief. When the Psalmist declares, 'fools say to themselves, "there is no God" ' (Ps 14:1), he does not imply that atheism cannot be defended intellectually. He means that anyone who believes that by getting rid of God he has rid himself of all gods is foolish. Those who do not worship the true God (verse 2) are not free not to worship, but are bound to commit themselves to another god (another entity which commands their allegiance): for example, a revolutionary ideology or the pursuit of financial gain. This is the inescapable alternative to belief in God. The Bible, with extreme frankness, calls it idolatry.

Real intellectual integrity demands that we are willing to be changed by the message, as we discover who we really are and how we ought to live. Such an attitude is a condition for understanding what the Bible means. Needless to say, we are not required to make up our minds before we have listened. Nor has anyone else the right to say, 'I have done the listening for you – this is what you must believe.'

3 Knowledge of the Bible's main points

Four cardinal points which the Bible makes form the basis of all our attempts to apply it to our lives and society. First, the entire physical universe and all life within it has been created by God, and fashioned according to his plan. Neither it nor human beings are the result of chance. It is not eternal or controlled by impersonal forces. The Creator is not absent. He sustains and allows all that happens.

Moreover, he is separate from what he has created. He is greater than the sum total of all that is. He has also given natural, moral and spiritual laws by which the universe functions. Real freedom for all God's creatures is only possible in so far as they diligently observe those laws.

Secondly, human beings have brought evil into God's Creation by making use of the relative freedom they have to deny the reality of God, arbitrarily to change his laws and set up other rules in their place. Sin is the creature defying the Creator, deciding that his own views and ways of acting are superior.

Sin is not, of course, to be confused with breaking society's conventions, values or traditions. These change. Breaking them may be right and necessary. What is repudiated in one generation may subsequently become thinkable, acceptable, legal and finally actively promoted in a later one (such as equal rights and rewards for men and women). However, God, not humans, is the arbiter of right and wrong.

Thirdly, God has devised a plan of salvation which takes in the whole universe. He intends to make all things new, bringing harmony where there is conflict and healing where there is disease. People need first to be restored to fellowship with God. They are guilty in rejecting God's authority over them. This is the primary problem of all human beings without exception; one they cannot solve on their own. They cannot make reparation for their guilt, nor devise any political or social solution to their loss of freedom. Human beings in choosing not to serve God choose to give up the only freedom that matters – the freedom to be truly human. They cannot pardon themselves or earn forgiveness. They can only cast themselves on God's mercy and accept the way out of a sinful existence offered in Christ's death and resurrection.

Fourthly, God is directing the whole human enterprise to a final climax. He will bring the present world to an end. He will judge and condemn all evil and vindicate the right and the good. He will then inaugurate a new heaven and a new earth in which his perfect love and justice will reign undisturbed.

The effects of this final salvation will begin to show themselves already in human lives and society before the end. Those who recognise God's justice and love will want to manifest them now in this life. In the power which God gives they will fight against every kind of evil.

These four points are only sketched in outline here. The Bible presents them in a number of different ways. Each writer has his own particular way of expressing God's fundamental reality and his dealings with human beings. The diverse richness of the language they employ needs to be fully explored. At the same time, the variety builds into an impressive unity. Careful study shows that the differences do not amount to actual disagreement. The message of God's revelation does not contradict itself.

4 Acknowledgement of the gap between two points of time

The Bible was written a long time ago – anything from 1,900 to about 3,000 years. The world has vastly changed during that time. Change has been caused partly by the impact of the Bible itself, partly also by technological discovery, the development of human institutions and the interaction between contrasting cultures, religions and ideologies. Whatever the cause, as we look at the text we should give due weight to the different ways of looking at life which existed then and exist now.

There are many laws, customs, institutions, sayings and cultural traditions in the Bible which today's world can neither easily understand nor accept. A renowned example concerns regulations about women covering their heads in New Testament times. Also, few Christians today refrain from eating meat containing blood (Acts 15:20). If we mistakenly assume that the two worlds are very similar, and that it requires little effort to move from one to the other, we will probably fail to do justice to either. In the work of applying the Bible to our reality, then, it is imperative to understand each world in its own terms. Each, in its different way, is the result of particular historical circumstances coming together. Each must be allowed freedom to speak for itself in its own language, before the two are brought together.

Anyone is capable of listening carefully to both worlds, one at a time. In practice, however, not many are good at bridging the gap between the two. Those familiar with the Bible and its living world may be reluctant to spend time digging beneath the surface of our modern society, either distrusting the modern tools of interpretation or else assuming that the Bible is already a perfectly adequate means of understanding the world that surrounds us. Conversely, those familiar with modern methods of uncovering the nature and functioning of our existence (sociologists, psychiatrists, anthropologists, economists and others) tend to dismiss the biblical view as archaic and non-empirical. If the application of the Bible is going to work, both sources of knowledge need to be used.

5 The use of the social sciences

The previous section leads to a consideration of modern ways of understanding the world, much of which we have fashioned according to our wisdom and felt needs.

Within the last century and a half a number of intellectual disciplines have been devised which help to expand our knowledge of both individual and corporate human life. Each covers a particular area of research and analysis, though there are many overlaps (eg between sociology, political science and political economics). They may be said to have three major interests: an investigation into the history of institutions and the development of the human psyche (in the case of psychology); an examination of the way in which different parts of society work or the reasons why they cease to function adequately; and a projection of possible trends into the future.

Much can be learned from these disciplines as they build up and systematise other people's observation and interpretation of phenomena. They take us beyond our limited and anecdotal experience of the world, exploring beneath the mere appearance of things. If we believe the gospel of Jesus Christ speaks to every aspect of human life, then we have a self-evident responsibility to set this life within the complexity of our particular society and culture. To understand our context we need to avail ourselves of every tested method of gathering and assimilating facts.

At the same time, the student of the Bible will use the social sciences with caution and discernment. What experts say about certain issues needs unpacking. If, for example, one wanted to grapple with the causes of unemployment and asked first a Marxist and then a monetarist their opinions, they would give conflicting answers. They might agree about the extent of unemployment and its distribution across a nation. They would not agree, however, about the reasons for its existence, and even less about its solution. They would be working from different theories concerning how humans interact in society and how political and economic power works. The Marxist passes all his observations through the grid of the class struggle, the basic and continuing antagonism between the owners and producers of wealth. The monetarist tends to work with an economic model in which the interests of all members of society can be harmonised through the unfettered working of market forces.

Behind the theories are fundamentally different perceptions of reality. It is imperative, as we listen to the arguments of social scientists, that we carefully explore the assumptions about human nature which are accepted as the basis for whatever results are produced. It is vital to scrutinise the process of reasoning which leads to certain conclusions, for every theory has behind it a commitment to some philosophical or ideological belief. We have to learn to test the validity, or otherwise, of these beliefs against the teaching of the Old and New Testaments.

6 The place of biblical scholarship

Alongside the rise of the social sciences, new approaches to the study of the Bible have come into existence since the early part of the nineteenth century. They entail a particular method of rational, historical criticism, and the belief that the Bible is to be treated like any other piece of ancient Near Eastern literature and that the origin and development of its books should be investigated with the utmost rigour.

Like no other writing, the Bible has been subjected to minute analysis. The main purpose has been to discover how each portion of each book relates to the background from which it comes. Biblical scholars have been particularly concerned with tracing the causes which have led to the present shape of each book, conditioning and informing the theological arguments of the various writers.

In order to facilitate this process of analysis, scholars have developed certain methods of interpretation. Starting with an analysis of vocabulary, grammar and syntax, scholars believe they have uncovered, in the case of many books of the Bible, a variety of written or oral sources. They then classify these sources according to certain theological traditions which they believe they can detect. They set the traditions within the likely historical context in Israel or the early Church from which they sprang and trace the history of their probable development into their present form. Finally, they assess the editorial work of the ultimate author of each book to discover his theological interests and the purpose for which he wrote.

Biblical scholarship has worked under the influence of the natural sciences, in the belief that the real meaning of the Bible can only be discovered by breaking the text down into its smallest component parts and subjecting each to dissection under the microscope. Scholars assume that the message of the whole is the sum of its dismantled and reassembled parts.

In principle, there can be no objection to a careful analysis of the text of the Bible. In particular, close attention to grammatical forms, literary style, kinds of literature, types of speech and the historical context in which and for which the various books were written is indispensable for a right understanding of what they mean.

However, the methods of modern scholarship have not always been used themselves with sufficient rigour and self-criticism. Like any method, biblical scholarship proceeds by way of hypotheses, many of which, in the course of time, have tended to become sacred laws. Far from being tested by fresh attention to the text, the assumptions have often determined the results which are obtained. Without adequate evidence they have been converted into unexamined dogmas.

For example, certain kinds of study of the first three Gospels (particularly those known as form-criticism) give a classic example of the illegitimacy of some of the methods used. By making a comparison of the Gospels, scholars have sought to show by what process the various traditions about the life and teaching of Jesus have come to adopt their final form. Investigation has led many to believe that during their transmission the stories gradually become altered in order to promote beliefs held by different early Christian communities. In other words, according to this view the Gospels as we now have them are a mixture of traditions about Jesus, handed down orally or in brief written form, and creative editing and additional writing undertaken to express particular theological convictions.

However, it may at once be seen that this method adopts a circular argument: a study of the Gospels suggests that in the early Church a particular situation has given rise to a piece of tradition (perhaps a parable or healing story). This situation is then used as a criterion to evaluate the different sources from which the Gospel has been compiled. The method is fraught with contradictions, for the cause (the tradition) has been confused with the effect (the early Christian communities). In order for the theory to stand, it is necessary to prove what has been supposed. The evidence, then, is indiscriminately pressed into approving the hypothesis.

In other words, this and other forms of investigation are based on imaginative speculation about the life of the early Church which goes far beyond what the text actually says. Instead of clarifying the meaning, methods like these may set going all kinds of hares which lead nowhere. Added to this, much critical interpretation has been based on quite unfounded historical scepticism.

For these reasons, a student of the Bible needs to be cautious about accepting certain critical conclusions advanced by scholars. As in the case of the social scientists, he or she will want to know what assumptions have been made, by what process of argument conclusions have been drawn and how evidence has been handled. Unfortunately, some scholarly work has been spoilt by the acceptance of a view of the world in which miracles (as special acts of God) are considered impossible or, for some reason, out of keeping with God's nature. This position has particularly affected peoples' views about the historical credibility of the life of Jesus and the early Church.

It is imperative that no-one, attempting to understand the Bible, is mesmerised by erudition. On the other hand, used wisely, the detailed research of many exegetes should help us to a fuller understanding of many passages and the inter-connections between different parts of the Bible. Criticism is not in itself wrong, for it is a particular way of applying the mind. It all depends how it is used and from what set of beliefs it starts out. In this sense the critics themselves need to be criticised for not always being sufficiently critical of the assumptions they have taken on board.

7 The work of the Holy Spirit

This aspect of a right approach to the Bible has been left to the end because it is the most important. The Holy Spirit is called by Jesus 'the Spirit of truth' (Jn 14:16–17; also 1 Jn 5:7). He promised his followers that the Spirit would 'lead them into all truth' (Jn 16:13–15). Whatever else this might mean, it has to refer to further revelation about Christ and his mission, which the Spirit transmitted to the apostles. The Spirit also leads Christ's disciples in every generation into a right understanding of the truth (2 Tim 1:14; 2:15). Finally, he keeps the disciples practising the truth (1 Pet 1:22; Jn 2:4). Truth is the opposite of all that is false (Gal 2:5; 2 Cor 4:2; Eph 1:13), untrustworthy (Rom 15:8; 1 Cor 5:8; Eph 4:25; 5:9) and unreal (Jn 4:23; Heb 10:1).

The work of the Holy Spirit, revealing to us new aspects of God's revelation, helping us to understand and apply what we read and guarding us against wrong interpretations, is necessary for two major reasons. First, we are limited by our experience, our education, the cultural background we have inherited, our language, the pressing needs of our life and the confusions of our society from being able to have an adequate grasp of the full scope of what God has communi-cated. We are constantly reducing and limiting the vast sweep of God's revelation, both by making it conform to our confined horizons and by simplifying it so that we can manage it. We desperately need the Holy Spirit to expand our understanding and to make us recall aspects of truth we are in danger of neglecting.

Secondly, we are restricted by our prejudice and wilful ignorance. We don't know or understand, because we are afraid of what we might discover. Because the will has been challenged to engage in costly action and change, the mind develops ways of justifying false and misleading interpretations. Because we find it uncomfortable and humiliating to admit we have been wrong, we find any method available to demonstrate that our interpretation is right. So, we need the help of the Holy Spirit to remove the distortions caused by sin in our lives.

The Holy Spirit may act in a number of different ways. Perhaps the most important is through the community of faith. As God's people call upon the Spirit for illumination, and study and seek to apply the text together, cultural limitations and sinful biases are much more likely to be overcome.

The Holy Spirit was given to the whole Church to guide it into all truth. A good example of how this may take place is given in the consultation on circumcision and law-keeping recorded in Acts chapter 15. A controversy arose, so delegates from two principle churches, Antioch and Jerusalem, met together. They debated the issue (verse 7), listened to factual reports of how God had worked among Gentiles (verses 7–12), made deductions from their experience (verses 9–11; 14), and listened to the Scriptures (verses 15–18). James then formulated a proposition (verses 19–20), which was accepted by the rest of the gathering (verse 25) and received with joy by ordinary believers in the churches (verse 31).

Where churches are prepared to listen together to the prompting of the Spirit, they are more likely to arrive at the truth. No one way of discovering the mind of the Spirit can give indisputable access to the truth. We need to be wary of exalted claims, whether these came through the heirarchy of a church, the guild of scholars, or those with gifts of prophecy and interpretation. Sometimes the Church may have to wait a long time before it is certain that a particular way of expressing its faith or a specific course of action is correct. The Spirit may demonstrate his activity as Christians from different backgrounds and parts of the globe discuss the intention and application of the Bible, and move slowly towards a consensus.

II

A Sketch Of Politics

Discussing politics is like walking into a minefield. Many sectors of society, like businessmen, the farming community, trade union leaders and pressure groups of all shapes and sizes have strong vested interests in the political process. It is also invested with inflated expectations. In an age when the gods have been banished to the inner recesses of the individual's private life, people expect political processes to resolve the great issues of the day: freedom from hunger, want and violence, justice for disadvantaged and minority groups, good relations between nations, stability in world money and commodity markets.[1]

We tend to expend considerable energy in blaming governments for everything in society we do not like – from inflation to violence on the football terraces – suggesting that we believe politics has the right solution for every problem, if only politicians could find the right rabbit and the right hat. This is a dangerous tendency, for over-optimism in the power of politics to solve social problems easily leads, as a result of repeated failure, to cynicism and apathy and the consequent loss of a mature public involvement in political debate.

Paradoxically, strong confidence in political procedures can also lead to an almost opposite conclusion. Some, who have never held political responsibility, may come to believe that their programme is so obviously superior to all existing ones that it must succeed once they have the reigns of power. Further, it may provoke the delusion, common among political extremists of different ideological persuasions, that they have a mandate to see their policies adopted by any means, including indiscriminate violence.

The ease with which tensions, prejudices and unrealisable dreams invade political life at every level should cause us to pick our way carefully through the many pitfalls, misunderstandings and myths which so easily distort our judgements. Among Christians strong ethical convictions in the realm of political life may produce severe strains, if not complete ruptures (as in the case of the World Council of Churches' apparently undemanding policy towards the implementation of human rights in socialist countries). In approaching the subject of political life, chosen as a crucial area for testing our ability to relate biblical truth to modern life, I would like to put down two markers. These will help us to set the boundaries of our survey of politics in general.

First, political action is a normal, good and inevitable part of our existence as human beings. In the widest sense, it refers to those processes by which whole societies order their social existence as communities of people dependent upon one another. Though the means for achieving this is rightly open to debate, the process itself simply explains what has to happen for human life to unfold at all. I believe that politics would be necessary even if human relationships did not tend to degenerate into anarchy, for society as a whole needs representatives or delegates to make decisions on its behalf. In this sense politics is part of the order which God himself created, in which some people exercise particular gifts in the public realm on behalf of others.

Secondly, it is beyond the ability of politics to solve the fundamental problems which assail every kind of human endeavour. It is only the incurably romantic and eternally optimistic who fail to see, or will not admit, that greed, selfishness, violence and fear are endemic to every kind of society. Political life may check or redirect manifestations of these destructive tendencies, but it cannot ever wholly eradicate them. Much political debate surrounds the question of which particular expressions of social disruption (e.g. racial abuse, strike action, take-over bids) should be most carefully controlled and by what means. It also concerns the comparative importance of giving attention to the problem either of abnormality and corruption in institutions (through law) or in people (through education or propaganda).

1 The nature of political life

If politics generally has to do with the ordering of our social life as a whole, more concretely it is about the gaining, controlling and exercising of power within a specific human community. Because experience seems to bear out the famous saying that 'power corrupts and total power corrupts totally', most of us view power as a dangerous commodity. In theory, of course, it is a good gift. Everything depends on how it is used.

I would define power in two ways. Firstly, it is the *freedom* to make choices and act. Secondly, it is the *possession* of certain advantages. These may be wealth, or status in the community, or the right kind of relationships (the old schoolboy network), or knowledge and educational qualifications, or our social, ethnic and cultural identity. They may include inherent gifts of leadership, or the loyalty one can command in certain circumstances. In the last resort, power does include the ability to impose a particular policy or set of regulations.

If this definition is acceptable, we could agree that neither freedom nor possessions are wrong in themselves. They become wrong when they are available only to some people who seek to ensure that others do not have the same right of access to them as themselves. Power is corrupted in society whenever there are groups of people permanently powerless – those who lack benefits of any kind, who are restricted by the accident of their birth and are unable to effect any substantial change in their situation.

Power may be exercised politically at all sorts of levels. There has to be in any society a certain *geographical* distribution, or devolution, of power. The reason for this is the problem of managing all aspects of government centrally, especially in a nation with a large population, vast distances to cover or inadequate means of transport and communication. Devolution may also respond to a political ideal, namely the right of people who pay local taxes to elect and call to account local representatives.

Power may also be distributed through *institutions*. One of the highest ideals of Western liberal democracy, since the age of revolutions, has been the balancing of power. Theoretically, there are three different organs of political life, each of which checks the power of the other two: the legislative, (parliament) which makes laws, the executive, which initiates politically motivated legislation and carries it out (in the British system, the Cabinet and government departments), and the judiciary (the courts), who interpret the laws. However, in practice, there are constraints on the effectiveness of the balancing acts. The main one is the tendency of the government of the day both to limit or denigrate independent sources of criticism and to justify its actions by repeated appeals to well-worn shibboleths about economic necessity and national security. The checks probably work better in a presidential system of government than a parliamentary one. Thus, in the British case there is little to restrain a government with a large majority in the Commons from carrying through any policy it wants. The civil service, with its responsibility to advise ministers and carry out decisions, may provide some constraints (both in debate about policy matters and in the shaping of legislation).

Any government, of whatever political persuasion, finds it necessary to legitimise its use of power. This may be done in one of three ways: either by the ballot box, or by verbal persuasion (including the use of traditions and consultation) or by physical coercion. Owing to the rise of political consciousness and the advent of universal suffrage in the twentieth century, most governments would prefer to seek their legitimacy through a voting system. Even in those countries where a military coup has suspended constitutional rights, a permanent denial of popular elections is seen to be impossible (in 1985, for example, Brazil returned to civilian rule after twenty years, and Uruguay after ten). Even in exceptionally hard-line cases, military rulers look for some credibility through a referendum (e.g. Chile and Pakistan). In countries where a multi-party system of political life does not operate (socialist nations influenced by the idea of a workers' party, and some emerging nations in Africa for fear of increasing tribal rivalries), regular elections still take place with some measure of choice in the election of candidates. In East European countries, however, elections may be less about legitimacy than about political education and national cohesion.

Persuasion can take a number of different forms. It depends fairly heavily in modern societies on the amount of control a government has over the means of communication or, alternatively, the amount of support it can muster from independent radio, TV, newspaper and magazine coverage. All governments are dependent upon their ability to keep in touch with the public, explaining their policies and motivating people to accept them and carry them out. This is true even where no alternative political party is waiting in the wings to take over government.

When persuasion fails to convince people to accept their view of social existence, some regimes are willing to resort to the repressive use of force. The police and military may be used to intimidate all opposition by breaking up protest gatherings and by arresting or kidnapping, torturing and killing dissident leaders. Alternatively, a government may enact laws to curb the power of potential or actual protest (as in legislation to restrict the rights of trade unions, forbid the right of assembly, extend the categories of crime against the State or probe into people's private lives).

The policies which a government seeks to implement arise out of either conscious or unexamined value systems. In rough and ready terms these may be categorised as traditional, liberal or radical. In fleshing out these three tendencies, I am aware that there is usually some overlap. In real life distinctive groups fit into different slots on an imaginary line between extremes. They may even adopt a mixture of traditional, liberal and radical stances towards different issues in their manifestos, but few people commit themselves in practice to a pure political ideal. We also recognise that the meaning of the terms is approximate and depends to a certain extent on assumptions which already possess an inbuilt bias.

(a) Traditional values

The most appropriate metaphor to describe this model of political life is the human body. The body always functions in the same way. It grows and decays, and is born again in another generation. Likewise, political life follows a pattern of repeated cycles.

In a body each part relates to all the others. It functions properly only when every organ is sound. Healing comes not by killing the body off but by isolating and treating the disease where it occurs. Both the internal functions and external relations of the body are controlled by the brain – that is, from the top down. The brain monitors, arbitrates and decides the body's functions.

When confronting change a traditional political order will, as in the case of a transplant, either absorb it and continue functioning as before, or else reject it. It does not like to have to adapt its beliefs and organs to the change. The basic social virtues are order and harmony.

These kinds of order tend to be authoritarian or paternalistic – allowing little, if any, dissent or alternative expression of how society should be run. They spring from the elitist view that certain minority groups are destined to rule society for the common good.

Authoritarian rule (however benevolent it may appear in practice) is usually justified by appeal to the need to preserve the continuing social fabric of society against every form of alien influence from outside. Open discussion of the purpose and usefulness of certain traditions, customs and policies is not allowed, because the body cannot tolerate the hypertension produced by internal conflict.

(b) Liberal values

Liberal political orders (I have in mind not a pure form of liberalism, based on the principle of freedom alone, but actual industrialised nations which operate according to present 'Western' democratic principles) are analogous to the functioning of industry. They do not oppose change. On the contrary, their survival depends on their ability to adapt to technological innovation and outstrip competition.

A liberal society is based on an evolutionary view of progress. Each generation is seeking to build on and perfect the machinery it has inherited from the past. No one type of product is intrinsically superior to another. The basic criteria for evaluating them is their consumer acceptability and their practical performance.

Therefore, this type of society welcomes a certain amount of experimentation springing from competition between diverse political policies. Depending on circumstances, different kinds of solution may fit the needs of the moment. The important virtues are adaptability and the ability to function well.

However, a plurality of options can only be taken so far. Competition may easily become unresolvable conflict. If different parts of the machine are not kept working together, it will automatically seize up. The system, therefore, must be properly managed. Above all it has to be protected from potential 'Luddites' who long to smash the machinery because they do not like the owners.

Thus, within the apparent freedom of a liberal society to debate alternatives and then to change, adapt and perfect its operations, there is a marked tendency to believe that only one way of organising industrial life can possibly work. Great faith is placed in the inherent superiority of a free-market economy, given that the most dangerous feature of its machinery (the creation of inequality, which, if serious enough, could cause a breakdown to occur) is protected by the safety regulations of some form of social security.

(c) Radical values

A possible model for a radical society is the artist's canvas. Radicalism assumes that a society can be totally remade. The old canvas can be laid aside or destroyed when the picture is no longer pleasing. The artist can take another canvas and, from scratch, can create something new.

Revolution, rather than evolution, is the language of radical politics. When societies come to a point where conflict between different sectors is so far-reaching that the body politic can no longer contain it, they collapse and give rise to a new order. Conflict may, therefore, be the most healthy thing happening in a society. It should be promoted and extended as much as possible.

However, the radical model (whether inspired by left-wing or right-wing convictions) usually owes more to artistic imagination than to what the artist is capable of painting. The dream of the great masterpiece never seems to materialise. The artist continually spoils the canvas and has to begin again. He is probably unaware that the paint being used is defective. The salutary fact is that no *new* order has ever been created by the power and inventiveness of human beings. What may appear as innovation is often no more than a rearrangement of the figures on the canvas.

These three types of response to political processes continue to influence political debate in our generation. There is a strong resurgence of traditional values, moral and political, though often mixed with liberal economic policies, in the so-called 'new right'. In many ways this political force represents an impassioned reaction to the radical utopian politics of the 'left'. The idealism of the future is being replaced by an idealism of the past. Both are responses to the collapse of the claims made for a liberal society that it would produce sustained growth, universal welfare and meaningful work for all. We live, therefore, at a moment when the clash of political ideals is becoming more belligerent. Christians, for both right and wrong reasons, are being drawn into the fray.

2 The scope of political action

Whatever values particular political groups may adopt, once they are responsible for government they are obliged in a modern society to attend to a number of functions. At the risk of over-simplification we may say that governments need to act in the following areas:[2] the management of economic life, the introduction of legislation, the maintenance of law and order, the defense of national security, the provision of social services, relationships with other states, the setting of objectives and future planning. Some governments also feel obliged to intervene in industrial disputes in those sectors which are of strategic importance to the nation (e.g. the coal industry, ambulance and fire services, road haulage and the docks). Most governments will try to implement either the policies of a manifesto, on which they claim to have been elected to office, or (in the case of one-party states) a plan intended to cover the next four or five years.

All the tasks listed above have their controversial elements. For example, in the economic field a government is responsible both for fiscal and monetary policies. In the first case it has to determine the level of public spending, principally on defence and welfare. There are a number of difficult questions to resolve: First, how much should a government spend (its budget level)? Secondly, how should the spending be distributed between social security, health services, education, defence, law and order and nationalised industries? Thirdly, should the government try to balance the books, only spending what it receives through direct and indirect tax – or should it be prepared to borrow (as does industry), in order to create new jobs and thus play a part in the creation of wealth? If it does decide to run a deficit by borrowing, how should the money be raised? (The usual methods are either through international finance agencies like the IMF and the World Bank, or through printing additional money).

Monetary policy has to do with the regulation of the amount of money circulating in the economy at any given time. This amount is usually measured by the quantity of coins and notes issued plus current accounts on which cheques can be drawn. In some definitions of the money supply all deposits held by individuals or institutions are also included. Governments cannot easily control levels of money in the economy. However, they can print or refuse to print additional money. They can also partially influence the amount of borrowing by raising or lowering interest rates, with the effect of either deflating the economy or, alternatively, of stimulating investment and growth. Monetary policy is linked to the government's perception of what is an acceptable level of inflation, and what are the main ingredients necessary for the economy's healthy and sustained growth.

Another major economic consideration which governments face is the exchange-rate of the national currency. Should a government allow market forces freely to determine the level, through buying and selling 'on the spot' and in 'forward exchange' markets, or should it intervene either by raising interest rates to attract money deposited overseas, or by direct legal measures to fix the rate and eliminate parallel markets? Governments also have to decide whether to fix or negotiate a prices and incomes policy in order to control inflation, and whether to protect home industry against cheap foreign imports by introducing either quotas, tarriffs or both.

Managing the economy is a hazardous enterprise. Whether or not governments have strong ideological convictions which incline them either to promote a mixed economy or to intervene in directing investment or to pull back and trust private initiative to generate wealth, they are all under constraints which come from the international community. Moreover, most economic policies seem either to produce contradictory results or by curing one ill (inflation) cause another (unemployment), irrespective of the economic wisdom being pursued.

A market economy is particularly susceptible to how individuals and groups (e.g. boards of industry, banks, financial houses and pension funds) perceive their best interests. In socialist economies economic life is dependent both on the efficiency or inertia of the party bureaucrats, who have to implement goals set by the party officials, and on the work-force's level of motivation to raise production levels.

The seductive notion, first propagated by Adam Smith, that by maximising the economic interests of each individual all others will be equally benefitted, is not true to real life. Interests conflict. Economic problems, therefore, spring ulti-mately from personal selfishness, low motivation to work and the imbalance in the economic power which different sectors hold. Governments can do little about the first problem, except to rein in some of its worse consequences, and can only influence and change the other two in a limited way.

Economic life is absolutely fundamental to the life of a community and, in one way or another, influences every other responsibility of government. Welfare provision is directly affected. Cuts in public spending, for example, will mean inadequate resources for education and training, causing a decapitalising of managerial and inventive skills for the future. This loss will in turn lower a nation's competitive ability against its industrial rivals. The inevitable conse-quences will be a lower economic performance. Thus each of these knock-on effects produces a further downward twist in the spiral of decay.

Likewise, cuts in health care can be counter-productive. Short-term savings may cause a long-term deterioration in the nation's general level of health. As work will be lost as a result, and as curative medicine is much more costly than preventative, such retrenchment will be a false economy in the long term.

Massive and long-term unemployment may cause anger and frustration which lead to unrest or even violence, especially among groups who feel particularly discriminated against. The breakdown of public order has economic impli-cations for a nation (as the 1984–5 coalminers' strike in Britain amply demonstrated). Conversely, lack of job oppor-tunity may engender cynicism, despair and apathy, effectively killing off (particularly in young people) the motivation to work. A fatalistic attitude to life negatively affects production and, therefore, the community's level of economic performance.

Finally, relationships with other states often hinge on economic considerations. For example, Western nations have for a long time refused to use the threat of disinvestment in South Africa to bring pressure on the Pretorian government to dismantle apartheid. The opening of China's potentially gigantic market to the West and her perceived need of Western investment and technology have been strong factors pushing China and Britain to agree on terms for the decolonisation of Hong Kong in 1997. The enormously profitable trade in arms powerfully influences governments to decide what kind of relations they want to maintain with one another as either suppliers or purchasers.

3 The main political issues

All political life is about goals and the means to achieve them. Political debate revolves around conflicts between goals or between means or between one and the other. It may also concern choices between greater and lesser goods, or between degrees of austerity and misfortune.

As we have already emphasised, the goals and to a lesser extent the means will be established according to whatever ethical values predominate in a culture at any one time. Values spring from a given perception of the nature and meaning of human life. This is the point at which politics links most obviously to the message of the Bible. It would be wrong, therefore, to imagine that political strategy and action is a matter merely of pragmatic calculation, divorced from ethical considerations.

(a) Democracy

Although it would be hard to find a definition of democracy which satisfies every shade of political opinion, everyone believes it is a good thing. Some form of autocracy, seemingly the only viable alternative, is no longer acceptable in an age of mass mobilisation. Democracy, based on universal suffrage and the equal value of each vote, is a very recent development, springing initially from the imposition of taxation to pay for war (no taxation without representation).

Two main principles stand behind democracy: first, *participation* – the election of representatives, who theoretically could be anyone, to carry out the work of government; secondly, *accountability* – political authorities have to be institutionally responsive to the wishes of the populace. Periodic elections, the main engine of democracy, hinder the formation of self-perpetuating oligarchies. Democracy is popular, because it seems to be the best defence against arbitrary rule. Nevertheless, democracy is not uniform across the globe. Western liberal democracies allow competing parties, while socialist and many Third World states restrict government to one party, although each constituency may have several candidates representing different factions within the same party.

The West's criteria for democracy may be procedurally correct, and yet 'rule by the people' may be a sham. Where proportional representation is absent (as in Britain), the preferences of voters are not truly mirrored in the elected assembly. Where office is dependent on economic patronage (as in the USA), the exercise of political power is only open to a small minority. For this reason socialist states claim for themselves a greater degree of genuine participation and representation, especially at a local level (for example in neighbourhood councils) than liberal democracies. On the other hand, genuine open debate about alternative policies is stifled, because it can only take place within the narrow confines laid down by one party. No independent group may advocate or seek to implement sweeping changes. Thus a centralised socialist system may easily become reactionary. All the more so, if it believes history is automatically heading in a certain direction.

(b) Freedom

The liberal democracies of the West have been shaped by a belief in the inviolability of an individual's rights. The pendulum swung, at the end of the eighteenth century, from the absolutism of rule by monarchs, (notably in France and North America, later in South America) to an individualistic view of political life. The State's primary task became that of defending and promoting the individual's right to pursue his or her own personal well-being.

In particular, the State was called upon to protect the absolute right to own property privately. This was seen as a supremely important guarantee of an individual's freedom from interference by the rest of the community.

Freedom was also associated with the right to choose personal values and goals, rather than being made to conform to religious or political dogmas decided upon by some external authority. The State was, therefore, also expected to guarantee the individual's right to be free from beliefs established by law, with the consequence that nonconformists, agnostics and rationalists should have access to the same educational opportunities as members of the State Church.

In our day, the passion for freedom has extended to the area of the conception of life. Militant pro-abortionists claim an absolute freedom for the mother to decide whether a foetus should be brought into the world or not. In this case freedom seems to be identified with personal convenience.

The modern liberal notion of the exercise of freedom ignores two important facts about human life. First, that human freedom is circumscribed by the reality of human nature. Freedom which seeks to remake the human image leads to confusion and bondage, for it constantly strikes against the constraints imposed by having to function properly as a human being (a creature made in the image of God). Secondly, different freedoms conflict. One person's freedom is another person's loss of freedom. In a world of limited natural resources not everyone can be equally free to consume without restraint. If some continue to insist on their inalienable right to accumulate wealth, they will have to ensure that others' rights to do the same are restricted. Hence, the liberal belief that freedom entails the absence of coercion cannot be universalised. And because freedom can no longer be conceived of as an absolute value universally available to all, it is either spurious or arbitrary. The State, therefore, is obliged to limit the freedoms of some people in order that those of others may flourish. For example, the freedom of some to buy and sell seven days a week conflicts with the freedom of others to enjoy a different environment on one of those seven days. Society as a whole has to make a choice between the two.

(c) Justice

In order to have some criterion for judging between different freedoms, the question of justice has come to the fore in recent years.

Modern apologists for justice, borrowing from the Christian tradition, assert that we must recognise that other people, belonging to the same species as ourselves, are worthy of the same respect we would wish to receive. Justice means ensuring that each individual is enabled to live a dignified life, developing to the full his or her creative potential. So justice is frequently seen in terms of inalienable human rights – that is, what I am owed as a human being, if I am to fulfil my destiny.

The basis for justice has been developed (principally by Rawls[3]) from a notion of fairness. It is a kind of sophisticated commentary on the 'golden rule' that we should act towards others as we expect them to act towards us. To avoid equating justice with my interests, I have to imagine I am responsible for drawing up the principles of a social contract, being ignorant of whether I would benefit or lose by the system. Assuming that I might receive the worst possible outcome, I would think it only fair that resources and opportunities be distributed equitably. Inequality rather than equality needs, justifying: 'inequalities can be justified only if (they) can be shown to be of positive advantage to the less advantaged.'[4].

Justice, then, is interpreted fundamentally as a redistribution of wealth and power in society, in order that the imbalance created by freedom should be smoothed out and equality between people restored.

Many political commentators believe that the pursuit of justice is the chief aim of politics today. The task of government is to arbitrate between the claims of rival pressure groups, favouring whenever possible the needs of the non-achievers and minority groups in society. This sounds fine as an ideal. However, those who exercise political power are not disinterested people. They are often expected to defend the best (unjust) interests of powerful groups in the community, and may consider this an expedient policy to pursue. Politicians in any political system are working under the constraint of sectional pressures, which can easily drive them to compromise what ideals they may have.

(d) Efficiency

One constantly hears the argument that political stability depends upon the economic performance of a nation. Where a nation is creating wealth at a sufficient rate for the majority of a population to benefit from it, its system becomes acceptable. The fabric of society may begin to disintegrate, however, when the economic performance of a society is in steady decline.

In a highly competitive world wealth creation through sustainable growth depends greatly on efficiency. Efficiency is taken to mean wise investment, forceful marketing, the careful use of the right technology, the cutting of costs and, above all, a hardworking and cooperative workforce. Over-manning and restrictive practices sound the death-knell for efficient industry and therefore for economic growth. In this context government has a responsibility to create conditions which allow industry to eliminate inefficiency from its operations; (e.g. by passing legislation to curb the powers of Trade Unions).

This argument for efficiency sounds plausible. However, it ignores two substantial facts of life. First, economic growth and wealth-creation cannot be ends in themselves. Efficiency must have a wider purpose than to produce a higher rate of GNP. The drive for economic growth raises expectations that will never be fulfilled. What is intrinsically open only to a minority becomes desired by the majority. 'Middle-class' objectives out distance 'middle-class' opportunities. The tail of an imaginary marching column never catches up with the head. To put the reality a little more crudely: if the system is going to be stable, not everyone can be equally greedy. Therefore, secondly, greater efficiency may lead to greater instability as the frustrations of the majority multiply. This may in turn lead to social unrest and impede the very growth on which the system depends. Without a conscious attempt on the part of a government to implement a policy of distributive justice, growth, as an outcome of greater efficiency, will become self-defeating.

(e) Security

Any political order is, naturally, going to pay particular attention to its own survival. It will, therefore, exert time and effort and deploy large sums of money to prevent a situation from arising which would endanger the continuance of the system in its present form. National security is the name of the game.

A state can seek to maintain its existence either by using a velvet glove or an iron fist. The velvet glove is the attempt to secure social cohesion through non-coercive means in our modern societies, mainly the educational system, mass means of communication and agencies (like religious bodies) which prescribe moral norms. In many societies, though probably progressively less in the Western world, the family also plays an important part in teaching a child to accept a 'normal' view of life. Nevertheless, no society can maintain one single value system (particularly if it has tinges of the 'traditional' about it), when education itself and the free interchange of ideas have produced a bewildering variety of views.

A government may have to tackle a situation where the velvet glove no longer works. Sizeable minorities (because they are no longer prepared to accept the arguments or explanations offered by the politicians in power) may resort to either non-violent or violent extra-parliamentary activity to express their political disagreement with existing programmes. In recent years such issues as work and unemployment, the deployment of nuclear armaments, the restriction of civil liberties and the secrecy of government have led to mass open-air protests.

It is probably true that most governments over-react to what they believe are threats to security. Where consensus is seriously disturbed, a state inevitably becomes more authoritarian. The drift may be gradual and, therefore, largely imperceptible. There will, however, be a number of manifestations: the police will be given greater powers to stop and search, arrest and detain, and exercise surveillance techniques; opposition to freedom of information will grow; the right to industrial action will be curtailed; representative government at the local level will be reduced or abolished altogether. Contrary to accepted liberal thinking, increasing freedom for market forces is quite compatible with decreasing civil freedoms, indeed the former may be a direct contributory factor to the slow ebb of individual rights. So a free-market economy is not only no guarantee of political freedom, but in certain circumstances it may actually promote a situation where liberty has to be restricted.

Notes

1   Leslie Newbigin, *The Other Side of 1984.*
2   Cf John Dearlove and Peter Saunders, *Introduction to British Politics* (Cambridge Polity Press, 1984).
3   Rawls *Theory of Justice* (OUP).
4   Bernard Crick, 'Equality' in Ben Pimlott, *Fabian Essays in Socialist Thought* (London, Heinemann, 1984) p.159. He goes on to say: 'Some inequalities can be justified, many not – particularly if one adds the vital condition of democratic citizenship: actually to ask the disadvantaged and to depend upon their reply.'

III

A Confusion of Voices

If students of the Bible readily agreed about how to apply the text to modern life, there would be no need to discuss the issues raised in this book. However, as anyone can quickly see, there is not much agreement about how to relate the faith of the Bible to the complexity of opinions, programmes and strategies in the world of politics.

Therefore, before we embark on a detailed study of biblical interpretation, we will discuss some of the reasons why Christians come to different conclusions, although they are using the same text.

I will outline some methods of interpretation being currently used and comment on their shortcomings. Then I will list some of the most important factors which help fashion the conclusions we come to, and also explain why Christians hold different opinions.

1 Ways of relating the Bible to political life

As far as I can see, three kinds of approach have been tried in recent years. I will call them 'literalism', 'analogy' and the 'second text' process. The name is unimportant, but what counts is the method employed in each case.

(a) Literalism

To explain what I mean I will offer one or two examples.
(i) Predictive prophecy Some Christian groups, often

described as 'fundamentalists', take passages from the 'apoca-lyptic' portions of the Bible (eg Daniel and Revelation) to understand current international events and to predict particular political events in our time.

The method characteristic of this approach is that of 'one-to-one': finding a definite and often exclusive relationship between the biblical symbols (e.g. the four beasts and the ten horns of Daniel's vision in chapter 7) and concrete events taking place (or about to take place) in the lifetime of the interpreter. The circumstances of Middle East politics have proved the most fertile ground for this type of interpretation.

Though the approach has caught the imagination of thou-sands of Christians, especially in America (some of the litera-ture has reached the best-selling lists), it is fraught with difficulties.

First, *there is the problem of not grasping the nature of 'apoca-lyptic' literature.* Literal interpretations take no account of the type of literature under review. Consequently, they fail to understand what is implied by the use of symbols (e.g. the wide occurrence of numbers). Failure to appreciate the purpose of symbolic language leads the reader to overlook the variety of ways in which language can communicate truth. The literalist method of interpretation ignores the cultural richness of different ways of writing, and perhaps even reflects an inadequate view of human creativity.

Secondly, *there is the problem of an unexamined nationalism.* Those who engage in the art of 'apocalyptic literalism' tend to be of a type. They see the universal struggle between light and darkness depicted in the Bible mirrored in the confrontation between enlightened Western forms of democ-racy and the totalitarian forces of socialism. More particu-larly, the struggle is between the USA, the supreme bastion of freedom, and the USSR, the chief example of a nation which suppresses it. Even more particularly, the struggle is between a certain sector of the Church and all who do not share their ideological outlook. Our popularly conceived national enemy has to be represented as the 'evil empire', a sinister foe from outside. It is inconceivable to imagine that the most deadly enemy of all could be a 'fifth columnist' which is perverting our outlook on the world from within. This way of applying the Bible hardly seems to leave room for measured self-criticism and national humility.

Thirdly, *there is the problem of historical proof.* The constant failure of the predictions to match real events never seems to daunt the literalists. They respond in two kinds of ways to the accusation that the predictions are no more than wish-fulfilments. They ingeniously rearrange the timetable for the fulfilment of prophecy and they accuse those who doubt the possibility of finding a highly specific relationship between prediction and fulfilment of denying the Word of God (the label 'liberal' is a convenient stick to use).

However, we ought to face the fact that the Old Testament relates the failure of prediction to false prophecy, and then look again at the real purpose of biblical passages which speak of future events.

Fourthly, *there is the problem of special illumination.* In order to be able to apply the meaning of numbers, beasts, plagues, human figures and so on directly to specific political events one needs a special insight. What is obvious to the 'apocalyptic literalist' is not obvious to other faithful students of the Bible. Hence, the suspicion that some claim to have acquired a secret knowledge of God's instructions not possessed by others. However, there is no objective criterion of interpretation by which we can test the validity of these views. Imagination and speculation are free to roam more or less unchecked. In the course of Church history claims to special knowledge have usually divided the Church and blown it off course from its main tasks (e.g. Gnosticism in the second century).

Fifthly, *there is the problem of ethical commitment.* Where it becomes a dominant method of interpretation, concentration on future prediction removes concern for the immediate world and its ambiguous political reality. The modern 'apocalyptic' approach to history assumes that every human endeavour only works out God's wrath and contributes to the final confrontation between God and evil at Armageddon

(Rev 16:16). Attempts to change situations of injustice here and now are seen as vain attempts to thwart God's decrees. Such a view, however, is the result of a distorted understanding of how God works in history. It is based on too pessimistic a view of human society and on too radical a separation between the final manifestation of God's kingdom in power at the end of history and its partial presence in the world today.

For all these reasons, we conclude that this way of relating the Bible to contemporary political events involves a wrong use of the text.

(ii) Absolute law Another school of thought believes that God's commandments should be directly applied to society, whatever cultural or historical variations exist. Some of these laws refer to personal issues, others have implications for society as a whole (such as Sabbath observance, understood – among other things – as a defence against the exploitation of labour).

Some people believe that society should openly reflect in its legal system the absolute requirements of God's moral law. They point out, quite rightly, that God's demands for personal and communal righteousness are not only applicable to those who acknowledge him. They are intended, as the only means whereby society functions properly, for all his creatures. Christians, therefore, should campaign for what has been called a 'godly' society.

This way of looking at the relationship between the biblical text and social existence seems proper, but there are some difficulties. Which commandments do we select as applicable to direct legislation? The criterion often seems to reflect different people's cultural and political preferences. Some Christians speak of 'Creation ordinances' as institutions or laws which are woven into the very fabric of human existence, and therefore should be implemented. By what principle, however, do we decide the range of these ordinances? Why, for example, should not the commandments of the Jubilee (Lev chapter 25) be incorporated into legislation (including the prohibition on usury and the remission of debts)?

Another problem relates to the ambiguity involved in trying to convert moral precept into codified law. What does one do specifically with a commandment like 'honour your father and your mother'? How does one translate 'honour' into administratable laws? It has often been stated, and proved in practice, that good moral precepts may make bad laws (e.g. the prohibition of drink or of adultery). In making laws we cannot ignore 'the hardness of our hearts'.

These questions raise two pertinent issues. First, what are the criteria by which some commandments are considered appropriate for legislative action whilst others are not? Unless the criteria gain a general measure of consent, the mere statement that a nation ought to live by God's law cannot help translate the biblical text into direct action. Secondly, do we not in practice (even if not in theory) find it necessary to place between stated Old Testament laws and our response to them a discussion of appropriate principles? In other words, we cannot by-pass the concrete nature of any situation by trying to implement the commandments as they stand. For example, when discussing the Jubilee laws in an urban environment we have to ask what is the *equivalent* of land?

The Bible, then, plays a fundamental role as a means to analyse situations, set the right course and inspire change. It does not give us ready-made blueprints to translate into action without considering the specific nature of the situation.

(iii) The claim of justice In recent years some Christians have become convinced that the biblical claims of justice can be spelt out in definite political policies. Other, opposing policies are assumed to contradict God's justice. According to this view, by reading the law and the prophets one can conclude that, for example, certain trading arrangements, taxation policies, price-control mechanisms, government investment procedures, immigration regulations and other political options explicitly conform to or deny God's way of establishing justice.

A variation of this belief asserts that the life of God's kingdom may be partially realised in concrete political terms in the present – the details can be found in relevant biblical passages. Those who deny such a simple equation are sometimes accused of evading the text's plain meaning for ideological reasons. Knowing what is just is not so much a logical question of applying the text of the Bible as an ideological one of either defending or letting go of one's vested interests.

There is enough truth in this viewpoint to make us pause before dismissing it as naive and unrealistic. The argument from justice helps to clarify political ends within a basic social perspective – namely that every society should give priority to achieving a dignified human existence for all those pushed to the edge of life. It does not, however, give us a ready-cooked answer about the right means to adopt. A direct, inductive approach to the text does not provide answers off the peg. For these we need to turn to a deductive process of interpretation. The following two methods are commonly used today.

(b) Analogy

Those who are convinced that an ancient text cannot disgorge propositions with an immediate political cash value today have to try to deduce principles of belief and action from general statements.

One example of this procedure is the debate about nuclear weapons. A nuclear pacifist (who claims that the use and/or deployment of nuclear warheads is immoral) is likely to argue from a text like Genesis chapter 18 (Abraham pleading for mercy on Sodom because of the righteous who dwell there) that the mass destruction of the innocent in a nuclear holocaust is an affront to God's nature. ('Surely you won't kill the innocent with the guilty – that is impossible. The judge of all the earth has to act fairly')[1]. He or she then uses this argument as one basis for opposing all employment (whether as first or second strike) of nuclear weapons, on the grounds that the mass-slaughter of non-combatants would result.

Pacifists also argue by analogy. Though they make much of the Sermon on the Mount, they do not base their case on any one passage. Rather, they argue from what for them is the most distinctive, authentic and original element in Jesus' ethic: 'love your enemies'.

The love command in the New Testament has three main strands: 'love your neighbour as yourself', 'love one another as I have loved you' and 'love your enemies'. Only the final one is unconditional. Jesus emphasises the revolutionary nature of his teaching by adding in the same context one question and one further command: 'If you love those who love you, what credit is that to you?', (or, 'How does that show grace working in your life?'); 'Be merciful, just as your Father is merciful' (Lk 6:32,36). It is impossible to have mercy on an enemy and kill him. Killing, therefore, implies a lower ethic than Jesus allows his disciples. In plain words it is plain disobedience!

Alan Kreider unpacks the meaning of the love command by reference to its original setting:

> In a violent situation in which expectant Jews were advocating a righteous war against the exploitive occupying Romans, Jesus came with something creative, with a message whose newness scandalised his hearers. 'Love your enemies!' . . . Love the Romans, love your atheist oppressors, love those whom you are tempted to resist by collective violence.[2]

By contrast, there are some Christians who would defend the use of nuclear weapons as a last resort. One such, Jerram Barrs, also uses analogy to press his case. He begins from the assumption that justice most clearly spells out the moral character of God. God's justice specifically requires that, both within a nation and across national boundaries, goodness is upheld and evil is eliminated. He argues further that the Bible recognises that sometimes wickedness is so great that punishment has to be overwhelming destruction (e.g. The Flood).

By analogy, the deterrent must be proportionate to the threats and the potential military power of an enemy, otherwise evil will be left holding sway. Barrs rejects that argument against nuclear deterrence which says that means used for defence should be in proportion to the ends desired, because he believes that on occasions, a nation's solidarity in evil may override the principle of non-combatant immunity.

The method of analogy argues from biblical case studies to universal principles and from these to contemporary events. We have only been able to illustrate it briefly. However, the way the method is used sometimes gives the impression that a person holding particular convictions is now searching for some biblical justification. The more general the principles become, the more likely this is, for such concepts as justice, love, peace and liberation have been filled with many different meanings. Analogy is a legitimate way of relating the text to contemporary issues. However, it needs to be directly related to the original meaning of the passage used. It can easily lead to wrong conclusions, unless there is a careful assessment of the precise points which are being compared.

Thus, those who defend, on biblical grounds, the possible use of weapons of indiscriminate destruction do not consider sufficiently two crucial aspects of their application of the text: first, overwhelming destruction was either ordered unequivocally by God or caused directly by him (our use of nuclear weapons would not be analogous to either instance); secondly, there is no way of being certain that the degree of wickedness today is equivalent in magnitude to that of the biblical narrative. The whole argument does not do justice to the uniqueness of the historical moment of the Old Testament.

(c) The first and second book

Many Christians, particularly in the Third World, have adopted a method which looks first at modern political reality and then at the biblical message for guidance. One writer, Carlos Mesters, speaks of his meeting with a group of Brazilian Christians in a rural area doing Bible study: 'They took hold of the "Second Book" (the Bible) and used it in every way in order to read the "First Book" (life). The important thing was life, seen and lived as a live expression of the Word of God'.

According to this method, appropriate Christian action is not discovered first from the Bible, though it provides a general reference-point, but from looking at some of the realities of life and using people's experience to understand what is happening. This process helps identify the relevant material to look for in the Bible, particularly those elements important for judging our practical commitments.

Both daily experience of the results of political decisions and detailed analysis of political theories, structures and policies are the first steps towards deciding how God's Word should direct our actions.

Undoubtedly this approach to interpretation roots the biblical message in authentic life and suffering, engendering an atmosphere of concrete reality. There are, of course, dangers to be avoided. The Bible may, for example, be used selectively. Instead of considering that the whole text may in principle be relevant to any given issue, the interpreter judges which passages appear to him or her to speak cogently to the situation. As a consequence, it is not difficult to predict which parts of the Bible will be quoted. But, in the process, the freshness and critical power of the text become stifled. When we allow the world to set the agenda, we may finish up hearing only the echo of our own voice, missing truths we need to hear.

Then again, reflection on political life and the way we experience it may become divorced from all that the Bible has to say about being human. We may be tempted to adopt certain tools of analysis without discussing, from a biblical point of view, their limitations and faults. We may allow certain ways of interpreting the functioning of social and economic life to occupy a position close to that of revelation.

In spite of adopting apparently divergent approaches to the problem of using an ancient text to speak to modern situations, these three methods have a certain affinity. Literalism, though it appears to favour a theoretical approach to political life and an approach to the biblical text which simply takes it at face value, does not operate in an historical vacuum. It is not hard to detect strong cultural and ideological assumptions influencing the literalist's application of prophecy to modern political events. The second-book process is not free from the dangers of proof-texting in a literalist fashion. And those using the analogical method can be selective in the range of Scripture they choose to consider worthy of comparison.

2 Factors which may produce divergent interpretations

The foregoing discussion has highlighted some of the conflicts over interpretation which exist among students of the Bible. It has also helped to pinpoint a number of factors which cause serious disagreements. We need now to draw these out, specifying the role which each may play.

(a) The pressures of culture

Cultures are formed by an amalgam of beliefs, values, laws, institutions, customs, language and art-forms. The various components are created over a long period of time and transmitted through family units, education, religious institutions and, more recently, the mass media. In a world of rapid transportation and widespread communication, cultures frequently come into contact with one another and, as a result, become modified. In many instances we find dominant cultures, aggressively promoting their values, alongside minority cultures, sometimes, (like Asian cultures in Western Europe), seeking to resist change or absorption.

The forms of culture are imbibed with one's mother's milk. As one grows, one accepts imperceptibly beliefs about hospitality, relationships between the sexes, duties to parents and children, structures of authority, ways of speaking, the division of labour in society, ownership of property and so on.

Many of these cultural factors will never be questioned. Others may be changed as a result of being pressurised by other cultures, or if people undergo a religious conversion.

Different cultural sentiments, such as the individualism of Western life, views about the place of women in society, work patterns, attitudes towards shame, honesty, the sharing of wealth and the process of decision-making will almost certainly influence what we believe the Bible teaches. Indeed, we are probably all predisposed to look for evidence in the Bible which seems to confirm the norms and practises of our culture.

(b) The force of ideology

Ideologies are accounts of the world which form the basis for the defence and promotion of particular economic and social systems. The word is often used in a negative way to imply the defence of vested interests. In this sense, ideologies are views of life which promote or justify what I, or my community, find preferable.

They are powerful forces which shape the policies of political parties and nations. They often pressurise people to conform to a particular outlook on life. Ninian Smart in his book, *Beyond Ideology*,[3] argues that ideologies function as substitute religions, 'for they mobilise deep sentiments and often demand great sacrifices; they give a sense of identity and purpose; they propound a theory of the world, a placement of men's lives in action and feeling'.

In our modern world two main ideologies compete for people's allegiance: free-enterprise capitalism and scientific socialism. They are both fundamentally secular in that they claim no ultimate justification from a reference-point outside the world. Both defend their beliefs by appealing to the necessity of the way things are. They are both pragmatic, pointing to their efficiency in promoting certain ends. They also have strong moral elements. Capitalism appeals to the notion of individual freedom and the fairness of receiving rewards for hard work, enterprise and risk-taking. Socialism appeals to the priority of achieving equality among all people by removing the monopoly over economic power held by one class in society.

These views are held passionately. In seeking to discern

what the Bible has to say about weighty matters like wealth-creation, ownership, justice, the poor, oppression, work and employment, sharing and the charging of interest, it is exceedingly hard to come to the text with an open mind, not already biased by the political and economic prejudices we have picked up elsewhere and which reinforce what we want to believe the Bible says.

(c) The right key

In may ways the Bible presents itself as a bewildering kaleidoscope of stories, laws, proverbs, prophecies, teaching, symbols, parables and metaphors. It also uses language which is not familiar to us from every day usage, some of it seemingly abstract and philosophical (e.g. 'fulness', 'principalities and powers', 'the Sabbath rest of God', 'the circumcision of Christ'). How do we begin to understand one part of the Bible in relation to other parts? How can we be sure we have not forgotten important teachings? How do we organise so many different parts so that they hang together?

These kind of questions and the feeling of confusion which underlies them have led biblical interpreters to look for one or more keys which will help to make sense of all the parts in order to fit all the pieces of a jigsaw together, we need the future to look at. Naturally, different ones have been tried: God's sovereignty, his convenant with Creation and with his special people, justification through faith, the kingdom of God, justice, peace, God's bias to the poor, the Incarnation, God's suffering on the cross, the Resurrection, Christ as Great High Priest, the Church and many more. Again, the choice has tended to produce different results in applying the message of the Bible to contemporary events.

All these aspects of the Bible's message are, of course, vitally important. It would be dangerous, however, to give any one more of a privileged place than the others, except as a helpful tool. However, in order to relate Scripture to specific situations it may be helpful, as a first step, to discover one particular key, using it as a touchstone of all our interpretation. We come to understand the Bible fully as we learn to see how each of these keys in different ways unlocks aspects of God's truth.

(d) The link between Old and New Testaments

Many people, trying to understand the meaning of the whole Bible, become confused about the place of the Old Testament in discovering and applying God's will to the modern world. What is its significance in the light of Jesus Christ? What difference does it make to have a Bible with two parts?

In one sense it is unfortunate and misleading that the adjectives 'old' and 'new' have been applied to the two parts, for it gives the impression that one is superseded by the other. Though popularly made, that would be a superficial judgement. It has sadly led many to neglect the Old Testament.

There is a clear historical continuity between the two parts. Israel's history in the Old Testament was marked by three covenants between God and his people. Two of them were implemented (with Abraham and with the Hebrew people at Sinai); one was promised for the future (in Jeremiah's prophecy). Israel's history in the New Testament speaks of the fulfilment of the first two covenants and the realisation of the one still remaining. God's promise to Abraham that in his seed all the nations of the earth would be blessed, liberation from slavery and the giving of the law ratified by the shedding of blood are all fulfilled through the death and resurrection of Jesus. Now all nations may experience salvation and the knowledge of God's perfect will.

The difference between the Testaments can be seen in two ways:

(i)   The universal extent of God's offer of salvation is now explicit. The Gentiles, who were a long way from God, have now been brought near. God's people are no longer identical with one nation or ethnic group.

(ii)   The significance of the nature and scope of salvation is deepened. In particular the New Testament speaks about the meaning of the death of God's Son in relation to human and superhuman powers.

The differences, nevertheless, do not negate the purpose and revelation of God to his people of former times. God always intended that the nations should receive his teaching. His concern for justice and mercy has always extended to all people. The salvation achieved by Christ is the fulfilment of all God's previous liberating activities. God's dealings with Israel, therefore, are not simply a matter of past history; they are to be seen afresh in the light of Christ.

Notes

1　Cf J R W Stott. *Issues Facing Christians Today* (Basingstoke, Marshalls, 1984) pp.89ff.
2　'The Arms Race: The Defence Debate' in J Stott (Ed), *The Year 2,000* (Basingstoke, Marshalls) p 37.
3　Ninian Smart *Beyond Ideology* (Collins, London) p 208.

IV

Making A Start

Up to this point we have attempted to do two things. First, we have looked in general terms at the range of issues that concern us in relating the Bible to the modern world. Secondly, we have pointed out some of the pitfalls which await us if we do not watch carefully. At this stage we should begin to look more closely at the mechanics of understanding both the Bible and our world.

The first text

Though it appears so obvious as not to need comment, the first principle for understanding the Bible is to begin with the text itself and study it from its own point of view. We could start by looking at the text from another person's point of view, dipping straight away into commentaries. Many move rapidly in that direction. However, to make this a first step is to become dependent too quickly on an external aid. If we do this we will find it much harder to develop and test principles of interpretation for ourselves.

Perhaps we should stress again that a right understanding of the Bible, in spite of the variety of interpretations, is not a utopian dream. It does not depend upon either intellectual ability or professional knowledge, though the latter on occasions will certainly shed helpful light on difficult passages. Faithful, biblical interpretation means strenuous and persevering work. There can be no genuine fruit if we are not prepared to dig and cultivate. The ability to work is not only given to a privileged few. Nevertheless, all too many Christians, used to expecting instant knowledge and pre-digested answers to their questions, are unwilling to spend the time and energy on learning and applying the necessary skills which will uncover the meaning of the text.

One symptom of this malaise is the emphasis in many sectors of the Church on the prophetic word. Though in itself one of God's good gifts and part of the Spirit's ministry by which God's people are encouraged, rebuked and streng-thened, it can too easily become a substitute for a Spirit-directed, rational reflection on the text. Under the guise of deep spiritual renewal, the prophetic word may disguise a new form of ecclesiastical authoritarianism, a communication from the Lord which should not be challenged.

This approach, however, like any which claims God's auth-ority behind it, needs to be firmly tested. God's Word is open to all of God's people. It is not primarily for self-styled experts, be they prophets, priests or professors. That is why individual Christians need to learn how to discover for them-selves the meaning of any particular biblical text and the message of the whole, without relying on intermediaries, however profound and honourable they may be.

Studying the Bible from its own point of view, means finding out all we can about the passage in question. As we work at discovering the original sense of what has been written, there are several basic things we need to do. We may call these our *exegetical ground rules*.

(a) Find out, where possible, about the author

The primary purpose of exegesis is to discover the author's intention in writing. It must help, therefore, to know as much as we can about the writer himself. In many cases this will be well-nigh impossible (e.g. the books of Kings and Chron-icles). In others we cannot be sure (e.g. Revelation – 'John' [1:1,9] might be any Christian leader). Or we may hazard a guess (e.g. Hebrews – the best candidate seems to be Apollos).

In other cases, however, there is ample evidence. If we take Philemon as an example (a short letter of Paul to a friend), we can learn a good deal both about the external circumstances and the internal feelings of the one who wrote. In the first three verses only Paul tells us that he was a prisoner, that he has a special relationship to Timothy, and that he knew Philemon well ('our dear friend and fellow-worker'). We may also note that, although it is his usual habit, he does not here call himself an apostle (compare Philippians and 1 and 2 Thessalonians). There are many other hints that Paul drops about himself in this short letter. You may like to explore some of these, asking what you can discover both about the man himself and about his circumstances.

Even where we do not know the identity of the author with certainty, we may still learn things about him. The author of Revelation, for example, had a close relationship to the seven churches of Asia Minor, suffered, like them, from some form of persecution and was on the island of Patmos (presumably in exile or imprisonment). Can we also deduce that he was allowed visitors who brought him news of the state of the churches on the mainland?

When reading through a book, therefore, make a note of any reference which serves to throw some light on the person who was writing. God chose to reveal himself through human beings, who wrote in their own style, out of their situation, as they were prompted by the Holy Spirit.

(b) Discover both the occasion and purpose of the book

Again we need to work through the internal evidence to look both for the actual circumstances which provoked the author to write and the purpose he wanted to achieve in putting pen to paper. Sometimes one or the other, or both, will be explicit (Romans is a good example – Paul tells us in different places why he was writing). In other cases the occasion and purpose will be implicit (Hebrews is an example, for we cannot be sure whom the letter was intended to reach).

With regard to the Gospels, it is difficult to know much with certainty about the background which gave rise to them. Nevertheless, both John and Luke (the latter in some detail) tell their readers why they wrote (see John 20:31 and Luke 1:1–14). The purpose of Matthew and Mark may be deduced from a study of the themes the authors emphasised and the way in which they presented them.

Both the occasion and purpose of Philemon are explicitly stated – the letter is all about Onesimus (verse 10). Paul gives us many clues which help to build a picture of the real life situation which caused him to write. To go through a book of this size, pin-pointing the evidence, is not a hard exercise. We learn the method best by doing it.

Where we have few explicit indications about either occasion or purpose, it is permissible to make an imaginative reconstruction, using the evidence that exists. However, where there are few real facts, we should be cautious about spinning out elaborate theories. Doubt about the historical accuracy of the Gospel accounts of Jesus owes a good deal to speculation of this nature. Many modern conjectures, which end up by recreating fanciful contexts for the writing of the Gospels, have rightly been portrayed as hypothesis built upon hypothesis.

(c) Look carefully at the immediate context

Such a ground rule obviously applies to a passage rather than to a whole book. The author's intention is often shown in either the preceding or following sections. One or two examples will show how this principle of interpretation works in practice.

(i) The parable of the prodigal son (Lk. 15:11–32) The immediate context is the situation told in the opening verses of the chapter. Jesus was condemned by the Pharisees and religious teachers for speaking to and enjoying the hospitality of 'sinners' – a class of people who by their deeds (sexual offences, collaboration with the occupying force, inability to fulfil the rigid requirements of religious rites) had put themselves outside of God's favour and virtually beyond

redemption. According to official religious views, Jesus had contaminated himself and was unclean. Therefore, his authority as a rabbi could be discounted.

In the midst of this situation of condemnation and conflict, Jesus 'told them this parable' (15:3). Only one parable follows, though told using three different illustrations. The point is that sinners are not lost, as the religious leaders assumed. They can be changed by God himself, who cares as much for them as for those who believe they are being faithful to his law. In the first and last story there is also a sting in the tail. The first ends with the words, 'righteous persons who do not need to repent'. The third is as much about the elder brother as the younger son. His relationship to his father was one of law and obedience, not of grace and forgiveness (15:29). In this way Jesus not only justified being with 'sinners' but also spoke a message to the Pharisees and interpreters of the law.

(ii) The temptation of Jesus (Mt 4:1–11) We cannot understand the significance of this event without linking it to Jesus' baptism (Mt 3:13–17), and in particular to the voice from heaven which says 'This is my Son, whom I love; with him I am well pleased' (3:17).

The temptation story is intended to show how Satan tested Jesus' understanding of his mission as God's Son: 'If you are the Son of God . . .' (4:3,6). The voice from heaven had confirmed to Jesus his special relationship to God. The words came from Psalm 2:7 and Isaiah 42:1. Taken together, the two passages show that Jesus was to interpret his mission in terms of being God's servant. God's purposes would be fulfilled by the servant voluntarily suffering death. Satan, on the other hand, seeks to persuade him to interpret his sonship as earthly power (being a miracle-worker, having political authority and enjoying the material good things of life ('the kingdoms of the world and their splendour')).

In other words, the voice at the baptism declared that God's authority over his Creation was to be claimed through death and resurrection (Mt 28:18), whilst Satan's strategy was to tempt Jesus to short-circuit his servant role of suffering.

(iii) A conversation with a former blind man and some Pharisees (Jn 9:35–41) In the context, this brief dialogue comments on an enacted parable. The story has to do with the recovery of sight as a picture of the conditions necessary for true belief (9:39). On the one hand, some among those who saw and heard Jesus are disposed to believe. The former blind man's own understanding comes gradually: the first step is, 'the man they call Jesus' (verse 11); then, 'he is a prophet' (verse 17); later, 'a man from God' (verse 33); later still, 'the Messiah' (verses 35–36), and finally 'the Lord' to be worshipped (verse 38).

On the other hand, some are disposed not to believe. Their attitude is summed up in verse 41. The blindness of the Pharisees consists in believing that they already see: 'surely, you don't mean that we are blind, too?' (verse 40). This is precisely what Jesus does mean when he says paradoxically, 'if you were blind . . . since you claim that you can see'. Refusing to recognise their myopia leads them to reject the very lenses they need to correct their vision.

(d) Interpret according to the kind of literature

In technical language types of literature are called *genres*. Different types communicate God's message in different ways and at distinct levels. The author may choose one kind rather than another, either because of his own natural inclination, or because of the nature of the subject matter, or because (especially in the case of apocalyptic literature) the circumstances of the writing suggest it would be the best method.

The choice of literature in the Old and New Testaments is basically between the following kinds.

(1) History Here an author relates past events in order to convey to subsequent generations a story which they should be familiar with (see Dt 6:20ff). The biblical writers were not professional historians in the modern sense of having a relatively dispassionate interest in the past.

They told the story on the basis of the traditions they received in order to convey a message to their readers. The past was significant in so far as it became a part of the present generation's understanding of God. The writers were selective in the material they decided to include (John tells us this quite explicitly – see Jn 20:30; 21:25) in order to cause the greatest possible impact.

Telling a story for a specific purpose and deliberately selecting some parts and not incorporating others, are approaches not to be equated with inaccuracy, as some biblical scholars have tended to assume. Scepticism has run so high amongst some of these that a biblical author is automatically suspected of misrepresenting the facts for apologetic reasons, until his reporting is cleared of historical doubt. Needless to say, this approach reveals an unsound method, for the fact that he is writing out of conviction is not a sufficient reason for being sceptical of an author's accuracy.

History can be neither retold and interpreted, nor doubted, except from positions of belief. Scepticism is no more free from belief than conviction.

(ii) Poetry In the Bible there are a variety of kinds. According to the normal way of classifying poetry in the English language, we can identify the following four types:
Epic or heroic narrative (e.g. Job and Ecclesiastes; perhaps Jonah)
Tragic (e.g. some of the Psalms – notably 22, 42–43 and 137)
Didactic verse (e.g. Proverbs and the so-called hymns of the New Testament Phil 2:6–11 and Col 1:15–20)
Lyric (e.g. the Song of Songs, Is 5:1–7, Hos 11:1–4)

Other cultures may possess other ways of classifying poetic forms which help to bring out further the rich variety of verse in the Bible.

(iii) Prophecy and apocalyptic For the sake of convenience these two types are often placed together, for they both seem to speak both of God's actions on an international and universal scale and of the future. At the same time, we should carefully distinguish them.

Prophecy is a word from the Lord announced through specially commissioned messengers (often chosen against their inclinations – e.g. Amos and Jeremiah). It is intended to accomplish three purposes: to lay bare specific evils committed either by Israel or by other nations; to warn them of the calamity which will come upon them if they do not change their ways (by renouncing false worship and unjust practices); and to announce the coming of a new age of peace and justice to be inaugurated by God's annointed servant.

Apocalyptic literature (such as Daniel and Revelation) does not believe that existing nations can come to a true knowledge of God. Instead, it tends to pronounce God's unconditional judgement on and destruction of the present world order with the creation of a wholly new universe ('new heavens and a new earth, where righteousness will be at home' – 2 Pet 3:13). In this sense, it is a commentary on the darkness of the existing times. It is born out of a period of intense violence and suffering in which God's people, like their Lord, are persecuted because of the sheer perversion of political and religious power.

This kind of literature in particular sees human conflict as an expression of the activities of invisible evil forces which challenge God's control of the universe. However, God's people can avail themselves of the victory he has already won over them (Rev 12.7–11).

(iv) Teaching material Passages with a didactic intention are usually found either in the letters of the New Testament or in its discourses (e.g. the sermons scattered through the book of Acts). Prose is the normal medium used, though as the biblical writers were not keen on abstract concepts, there are plenty of examples of metaphor and pictorial illustrations embedded in the material.

The extensive sections of law in the Old Testament might also be included under teaching material. They were intended to be learnt, memorised and put into practice – 'never forget these commands that I am giving you today. Teach them to your children. Repeat them when you are at home and when you are away' (Dt 6:6–7).

The division of the Bible into four basic kinds of literature is intended only as a guide to make us aware that it contains a variety of written forms. Each should be interpreted according to its particular way of communicating. It is especially important to distinguish between truth given in the form of straight propositions (e.g. 'Christ died for our sins . . . he was buried . . . he was raised on the third day . . . . he appeared to Peter – 1 Cor 15:3–5) and in the form of symbols (e.g. 'I am the gate for the sheep . . . he will come in and go out, and find pasture' – Jn 10:7–9). Knowing when to take a statement at its literal face-value and when to see it in symbolic terms is one of the most important clues to correct interpretation.

Naturally, many passages belong to more than one of these groups. Samuel's warning to the people of Israel (1 Sam 8:6–8), for example, contains history, prophecy and teaching. The transfiguration of Jesus (Mk 9:2–13) is history containing teaching in the form of discourse. *To each, then, the interpretation which corresponds to its literary type.*

(e) Interpret according to the writing devices being used

In each one of the following five cases truth is being conveyed through some point of comparison.

(i) A simile This is a simple comparison: 'as a hen gathers her brood . . .' (Lk 13:34); 'as a grain of mustard seed . . .' (Mt 17:20); 'all flesh is like grass . . .' (1 Pet 1:24); 'like a child . . .' (Mk 10:15)

(ii) A parable Usually a single point is being made by means of a more elaborate comparison. The original meaning may be decided according to a number of different factors:

The occasion – e.g. Luke 16:14, 'The Pharisees . . . sneered at Jesus, because they loved money.'

The introduction – e.g. Luke 18:1, 'Jesus told his disciples a parable to teach them that they should always pray and never become discouraged.'

The conclusion – e.g. Mark 13:37, 'What I say to you, then, I say to all: watch!'

The interpretation is already included – e.g. Matthew

13:18–23, 'Listen, then, and learn what the parable of the sower means.'

(iii) Symbols In some ways these can cause the greatest confusion in interpretation because people want to read too much in to them. Handled with care, symbols are powerful and down-to-earth ways of communicating truth. A symbol is one object which represents another. The following are some examples of how different symbols are used:

A person – the Holy Spirit is likened to wind, fire, a seed, oil and water.

A teaching – life is symbolised by a puff of smoke (Jas 4:14); blood symbolises the sacrifice of one's life (Heb 9:12)

A community – the Church is symbolised by a body, a temple, a bride, a new person, a flock and by many other objects.

An emotional state – the sea often symbolises threat and danger ('save me, O God! For the waters have come up to my neck' – Ps 65:7; 69:1).

(iv) Types the word is used in biblical interpretation of any institution, object, place or event which prefigures a truth revealed in a later period of history. The period prefigured, which usually refers to Jesus Christ himself or some aspect of his ministry, is often called an antitype.

Adam is specifically called a type (*tupos*) of Christ (Rom 5.14). Christ is also anticipated as a prophet by Moses (Acts 3:22), as a priest by Aaron (Heb 5:14) and by Melchisedek (Heb 5:10; 7:1–3), and as a king by David (Acts 13:22–23).

Paul argues that the Israelite people, saved from the slavery of Egypt through the sea, protected by God in the cloud and in the provision of water, were a type of the Church. Paul uses the historical analogy as a warning to the Church not to follow their example (1 Cor 10:1–11).

In another passage in the same letter to the Corinthians he illustrates the meaning of the cross and Resurrection by appealing to types (1 Cor 5:7). By following through the way the types are used, one can penetrate further into the rich meaning of Christ's self-sacrifice.

(v) Allegory This has a similar structure to a parable, except that many different points of comparison are being made.

It is a good rule never to use the Bible to allegorise unless the passage concerned obviously seems to demand it. There are, in fact, relatively few examples: the parables of the sower and the wheat and weeds (Mt chapter 13), and the comparison made between Hagar and Sarah. (Gal 4:21–31) are two. Another one might be Christ's discourse on the shepherd and the sheep (Jn 10:1–16), for he appears to be making a number of related points.

The danger inherent in the popular practice of allegorising is that of making the text perform a task for which it was not intended – that is, to disclose meanings apparently hidden in the text. The person with the greatest imagination and ingenuity can produce the most fanciful results. However, if the text does not itself receive an elaboration of every detail of a story, the process of finding corresponding meanings for each point may cover over or distort the original meaning. As modern interpreters we have no authority to add meaning to the text by our inventiveness where it is not obviously present in the first place.

(f) Discover parallels with other passages

The purpose of finding parallels is to build up a picture of a particular subject by looking at the way it is referred to at different stages in the history of Israel and the Church. Thus, for example, we may want to understand a frequently quoted text from the Sermon on the Mount, 'Blessed are the poor in spirit, for theirs is the kingdom of heaven' (Mt 5:3). To help us recognise who are the poor in spirit we need to turn to passages in the Old Testament, like Isaiah 57:15, 'I also live with people who are humble and repentant, so that I can restore their confidence and hope'; Psalm 34:18, 'the Lord is near to those who are discouraged; he saves those who have lost all hope'; Psalm 147:3, 'he heals the broken-hearted and binds up their wounds'; Zephaniah 3:11–12, 'I will remove everyone who is proud and arrogant . . . I will leave there a humble and lowly people, who will come to me for help'.

On each occasion a new dimension to the meaning of

'poor in spirit' is added. As a result of our search, using cross-references, we are able to say that Jesus has in mind a group of people who experienced certain adverse circumstances and who adopted a particular attitude to God as Saviour.

(g) Study the structure of the arguments

This is an important way of getting inside the mind of an author. It is particularly applicable to didactic passages. The purpose is to follow the line of reasoning, uncovering the assumptions and tracing the logical process from there to the conclusions.

In Romans chapters 9–11, for example, Paul wants to explain why his compatriots did not acknowledge their Messiah when he came. He assumes that God's Word cannot have failed, that the problem is not with God, for he has not rejected his people (9:6; 11:1).

Paul, building on this assumption, develops his explanation in the following ingenious way. First, the real Israelite is the one who has accepted Jesus, the Messiah, proving thereby that he or she belongs among the children of promise. Secondly, belief is wholly a matter of God's mercy; it does not depend on being physically descended from Abraham, the father of the race. God's mercy is free, it cannot be gained either by racial allegiance or by keeping religious precepts. God is also free in his exercise of mercy. Thirdly, a remnant of Israelites have always been faithful to his covenant. They are his true people. Fourthly, the offer of salvation through Christ is continually being made to all who will listen. Salvation is open to all 'who call on the name of the Lord'. The only thing they have to do is get rid of their self-righteousness. Finally, as a result of the Jews' rejection of Christ, the gospel came to the Gentiles, for whom it was also originally intended (10:19–20). The entry of Gentiles into the blessings of salvation may arouse Israelites to reconsider the foolishness of their unbelief and bring them to accept that God's purposes are finally fulfilled in Christ.

In this lengthy passage Paul develops an intricate theme,

not for the sake of a theological debate, but out of a pastoral and missionary concern for his own people. To understand its full significance we need to pay attention both to the main argument and the supporting reasons given to demonstrate it.

We have been trying to summarise in a few paragraphs the inductive method of biblical interpretation. In seeking to discover the author's original intention it focuses on the way the original languages work, the historical context, the literary form, a comparison with other parts of Scripture and the theological argument.

The value of the inductive method of exegesis is that *anyone* can do it, as long as they are willing to master the tools of the trade. Its importance lies in the fact that the meaning of the text is subject to some kind of objective control. We are, in most cases, able to distinguish with some confidence true from mistaken (individualistic and idiosyncratic) interpretations by carefully applying principles. As Peter says, 'no prophecy of scripture is a matter of one's own interpretation'. We are not permitted, in the current jargon, to 'privatise' the Bible.

2 The second text

Judging by the vast disagreements over most subjects to do with our world, there is no easy path to understanding the way modern human communities work. Unlike the first text, we cannot apply generally agreed rules to the interpretation of our daily situation. Nevertheless, not everything is confusion or a matter of pure personal opinion. There are means we can use to understand the nature and functioning of our society. Three kinds of tools are particularly essential: our own personal observation, systematic social analysis and theological analysis.

(a) Personal observation

Each one of us can cultivate a questioning and critical mind. We do this through reading, through personal experience of concrete situations and through talking to people who know more about the subject (say, local housing or government aid to Third World nations) than we do. It would be absurd to think we could begin to penetrate deeply into more than a small handful of issues on our own. The Christian Church, however, has the resources to cover just about every topic which regularly affects our lives.

(b) Social analysis

As the modern world is so complex, we have to rely on the expertise of professional observers. Whether sociologists, economists, political scientists or anthropologists, they have gone through a training which gives them a knowledge and ability to judge that most of us do not have. The social sciences, as they are called, have developed certain methods for observing, gathering statistics, measuring, interpreting and testing them and drawing conclusions.

Of course, the techniques are not free from bias. Whenever one is dealing with human concerns, there can be no such thing as totally objective and neutral methods. Each observer marshalls the evidence, selecting parts of it, discarding others and organising the whole according to social, political or even religious beliefs. None of our knowledge is free of the value-systems we have consciously or unconsciously adopted.

Nevertheless, social scientists have a grasp of the material relating to their speciality which most of us do not possess. Their work can provide us with three useful aids: additional knowledge of facts, a set of warning-lights to protect us from major pitfalls and a sounding-board to test our own ideas and observations against.

(c) Theological analysis

It is not possible to understand the human world without understanding the nature of humans. A Christian believes that no amount of rational investigation will ever uncover the two most basic things we need to know about human beings: that they have been created in the image of God and that because of sin they are cut off from God's life, which alone can heal and restore them.

There are basic aspects to human life which only these two hypotheses can explain: on the one hand, human beings need a sense of purpose, and possess a hunger for love, a disillusionment with material objects, and an intuition that life continues beyond physical death; on the other hand, they also have a sense of failure and frustration that human society does not work better, a sense of guilt and shame, irrational fears, the impulse to hurt even those they profess to love and the willingness to tell lies and to gain their own ends, even if it means using violence, corruption or false testimony to achieve them.

Christians believe that all of these attitudes and behaviours are an observable part of our daily existence. They also believe that no other explanation than that of personal creation and original sin does justice to the facts. Any social analysis which discounts these two hypotheses is reduced to asserting that human beings are no more than their genetic inheritance, the sum total of the culture into which they were born, the moulding influence of their family, the conditioning factors of their education and their own individual experiences. Though all these are powerful agents which shape our beliefs and reactions, they do not explain all that we sense about ourselves.

Though the analysis of any aspect of our life which ignores the facts of creation and sin may be correct to a point, it is ultimately superficial. To recognise these facts is vitally important when it comes to understanding either the causes of our political dilemmas or to suggesting workable solutions. We must be careful not to allow the Christian analysis to be discounted because it does not conform to a set of analytical criteria which can be verified in ways set out by existing scientific disciplines. This sleight of hand has been practised in our modern age in the name of science and rationality. Because it implies that the investigative powers of the human mind are the measure of all things, it has impoverished our understanding of why human beings behave as they do, leading us up many false trails and into many blind alleys.

Fathoming the meaning of our lives and the ways in which and for which the structures and institutions of our societies function takes place when we are able to bring together a number of social disciplines. Our own experience and trained observation also have an important part to play, whilst our beliefs will add fresh dimensions of understanding, and either clarify or else obscure what we see and hear.

V

Identifying The Evidence

The Bible can only speak to the modern political arena if its message has political implications. Owing to the influence of Western individualistic thought, the separation of the public and private spheres of life and a failure to see how the New Testament follows the Old Testament, many Christians believe the gospel has little to do with political life.

This book is based on an opposite assumption. It seems obvious to me that a person's inner life cannot be divorced from that person's circumstances in society. There is no barbed-wire fence between an inner and outer reality. All human beings are deeply affected by the human relations they are involved in. These in turn respond to social, economic and political forces which shape our expectations and lifestyle by determining such things as our disposable income, job opportunities, the quality of our children's education and the kind of housing we live in.

More important than our daily experience is the witness of the Bible. It is full of material which relates directly or indirectly to the social organisation of human communities. Three specific questions will concern us in the remaining chapters: *to identify the most crucial evidence where the biblical writers touch on political issues, to suggest ways of interpreting the evidence and to examine its significance for contemporary political life.*

These three tasks cannot be easily separated, for both the identification and interpretation of the evidence will depend in part on how we understand the political dimension in our modern setting. The Bible can only speak a genuinely prophetic word to our generation if it is first read with our particular political circumstances in mind. Forming an authentically Christian opinion on contemporary issues comes from travelling back and forth across the bridge from the biblical text to our world. It is a fascinating and sensitive task.

This chapter will address the first of the three questions, though it is impossible to offer more than an over-view of some of the material which bears on political life.

The Old Testament

(a) Nationhood

The Old Testament is largely about how God chose, cared for and prepared one nation to understand and commend his character and will to all the world he made. God promised Abraham that he would bless all the nations through him. The importance of this promise is emphasised by its four-fold repetition (Gen 12:3; 18:18; 22:17–18; 26:4; 28:14). It is taken up again in the New Testament (Acts 3:25; Rom 15:8; Gal 3:8). Through Isaiah God calls Israel to its missionary task, reminding the nation that it exists for the rest of the world's sake: 'I will also make you a light to the nations – so that all the world may be saved' (49:6)

God's concern with the whole world is born out by Jesus' final commission to his followers, 'Go, therefore, and make disciples of all nations' (Mt 28:19, RSV). This command immediately follows the statement that God has given him complete authority over the whole of human existence.

God made the Hebrew people into the nation of Israel, rescuing them from religious and political oppression in Egypt. The story of the Exodus is familiar and has been interpreted extensively as a political act. In the events leading up to Israel's liberation from Egypt we see clearly how God judged between two peoples.

The Hebrews' situation in Egypt was a classic one of

oppression. A powerful race used a minority group as cheap labour to create wealth for only a small handful of privileged people. The story spells out the evils of economic slavery, racial discrimination, attempted genocide and the constant physical violation of human beings.

When God responded to the people's cry and delivered them from the Egyptians' power he performed a political act. He judged one nation, condemning both the political ends and means of the Egyptians and formed another.

The purpose of the new nation had both a religious and social dimension. On the one hand, it had a responsibility to proclaim the nature of God who 'brought you out of Egypt, where you were slaves' (Ex 20:1), and to teach the way of true worship. On the other hand, it was called to demonstrate how a whole nation should live under God's rule. These two aspects of its life were welded together, just as the opposites (idolatry and injustice, from which the Hebrews had been released) were also united (see Rom 1:18).

So in important ways, still to be established, Israel was designed by God to be a 'model of nationhood.'

(b) The Law

The life of the new nation was regulated by the laws which God gave through Moses. These were ratified by the giving and receiving of a covenant in which God promised to stand by his people and the people promised to observe his laws (Ex 19:3–8; 24:3–8).

The laws were intended to show in detail how a liberated people should be organised as a community. They were directed towards individual behaviour, life in the extended family and the nation's conduct as a confederation of tribes (geographically distinct social groupings). The laws were designed in particular to make slavery, injustice and oppression impossible (Ex 22:21; 23:29; Lev 25:42) and to build a free and equal society. Without being able to summarise all their provisions, we can note some of the main characteristics of these laws.

First, God's people were to care specially for the weak in

society. Widows, orphans and immigrants were singled out for special mention. They were the most vulnerable, for they had no relation close enough to defend and protect them. Though it was easy for other people to forget them or even exploit their lack of power (using them as cheap labour), they had automatic rights (Ex 22:21–23; Deut 24:17–22; 27:19; Ps 82:2–4).

Defenceless people are the ones who, in God's eyes, determine the meaning and use of power and political responsibility in society. A society operating according to God's laws, therefore, is one where the dispossessed and disadvantaged receive preferential treatment, their needs being the first to be met. God requires compassion before all else, and abhors all policies and practices where some are able to take advantage of the impotence of others.

Secondly, the Sabbath and Jubilee laws made the personal accumulation of wealth for private ends at the expense of the rest of society impossible (Lev 25). Private, accumulated wealth shifts the balance of political power away from the community as a whole and concentrates it in the hands of a few. It creates and maintains an economic imbalance in society extremely hard to reverse and makes exploitation through control of the labour market and debt-bondage highly likely.

Behind the Jubilee law lies the question of the ownership and use of land. Like other laws, it relates directly to the Hebrew people's experience in Egypt. There, all land was held in sacred trust from the gods by the priestly caste and the king. They were, as a result, the monopoly owners of wealth in the nation. The situation in Israel is entirely different. The land is owned by family units on the basis of an equal distribution. The whole people is a nation of priests, called to exercise stewardship of the land which belongs in an absolute sense to God alone (Ex 19:6; Lev 25:23). The link between God, religious and political leadership and the ownership of wealth is emphatically cut in Israel, for the priestly tribe of Levi was not allowed to own land for itself (Deut 18:1–8; 12:12–19; 26:12).

The Law required, therefore, a regular redistribution of wealth to limit the economic power of any one sector in society and to give all groups an opportunity to contribute to the community's economic life.

Thirdly, the forms of punishment prescribed in the Law are socially important. These were either death (for particularly serious crimes), flogging or, much more frequently, repayment and reparation (Ex 22:1ff; Lk 19:8). Imprisonment is never mentioned. We can only guess at the reason. It seems likely that because of the loss of access to the goodness of Creation, the Israelites would have compared it to their life of bondage in Egypt.

The death penalty may never have been judicially carried out; its provision, however, demonstrated the ultimate seriousness of arrogating to oneself the right to end another person's life. Because God alone possesses this right, the death penalty can only be carried out if God directly sanctions it. Flogging is a physical punishment intended to demonstrate the seriousness of violating another's physical integrity. It would, therefore, be particularly significant in cases of unprovoked physical aggression. Reparation is a form of punishment, for the offender suffers a loss (of time and money). At the same time it makes forgiveness possible by bringing together the offender and the victim.

Punishment in Israel was the responsibility of the whole community. Indeed, even in criminal law a relation of the violated person, rather than the State, prosecuted. One of the major problems of internment is that society as a whole can conveniently forget its responsibility towards offenders against the law. By laying down both retribution and restoration as the purposes of punishment, the Old Testament Law seeks to maintain a balance between the dignity owed to the victim and to the criminal.

(c) The monarchy

Kings were introduced into the life of Israel at the time of the prophet Samuel, several generations after the founding of the new nation. For many years the national affairs of the people were administered on a sporadic basis, as the situation demanded, by elders and judges. Judges were appointed for a specific period of time. Their office could not be inherited. Gideon rightly refused the people's request to become king and set up a royal dynasty (Judg 8:22–23). He reminds the people that Israel is a theocratic nation, ruled by God alone (also 1 Sam 8:7; 10:10). On the other hand, Abimelech had himself proclaimed king and ruled for three years. His reign began and ended in violence. It was a foretaste of the troubles that a centralised political authority would bring to the nation.

Considerable doubt and controversy surrounded the initiation of the monarchy. The people, rather than God, took the initiative in requesting Samuel to grant them a king. The excuse was that Israel was experiencing internal anarchy because of the incompetence and corruption of Samuel's sons, Joel and Abijah. At the same time, the nation was in constant danger of attack from outside. It seemed obvious that they should have a king like the other nations (1 Sam 8:5).

However, the request was interpreted as a rejection of God, who had shown his faithfulness by liberating his people at the time of their greatest need (1 Sam 8:8). The people showed they wanted to protect themselves independently of God. The problem with monarchy was that it repeated the experience of Egypt and encouraged the theory and practice of the divine right of kings from which Israel had suffered. Thus, when Samuel warns the people of the consequences of having a king, he might have been speaking of the Egyptian Pharoah. Monarchy represented a return to the conditions of slavery (1 Sam 8:17). It meant the creation of a standing army, the centralisation of power, the beginning of a state bureaucracy (1 Sam 8:14–15), the raising of taxes to pay for military expenditure and the king's extravagant lifestyle (1 Sam 8:12–13). Finally, and worst of all, it implied that the king, counter to the ideal of a theocratic nation, had owner-ship rights over his subjects.

God granted the people the king they wanted, though the desire sprang from the hardness of their hearts. In one sense, because of its evil effects upon the life of the community, it was an act of judgement. In another sense, God tempered the judgement with mercy by laying down stringent rules to govern the extent of the king's power (Deut 17:14–20). He was to be accountable to God by adherence to the precepts of the Law, the priests rather than himself being the Law's official interpreters. The monarchy also became a symbol of hope, for the Lord promised to send one day a righteous king who would restore again the perfect theocracy (Is 32:1ff).

(d) Idolatry

Samuel states that Israel's disobedience in asking for a king was the result of forsaking the God of the Exodus to serve other gods (1 Sam 8:8).

In the Old Testament the exercise of political power is inseparably linked to a particular religious foundation for the well-being of the community. One reason why the events of the Exodus are so significant is that they show that God rejected the divine right to rule. The Pharoah was considered unique in that he alone possessed the image of the supreme god. As his son he had supreme authority and control over all aspects of life. The good fortune of every family in the nation was tied to their acquiescing in the continuing order of things. This order was holy and could not be broken without inciting the wrath of the gods, thus threatening the stability of society and bringing calamity upon the people.

In the story of Israel's liberation, the request of Moses and Aaron, 'Let my people go, so that they can hold a festival in the desert to honour me' (Ex 5:1), is profoundly revolutionary. The suggestion that there is another god to whom the king of Egypt has no access, one who demands the right to reorder society in the interests of a minority group, breaks Egypt's entire social order. The request had enormous political overtones, for it implied that the nation's unity under the king's supreme authority was not an absolute good.

It is not surprising that the king felt severely threatened, nor that he reacted by redoubling the oppression and trying to discredit Israel's leaders by denying the religious basis on which their request is made: 'make these men work harder . . . so that they won't have time to listen to a pack of lies' (Ex 5:9). It is not surprising, either, that full religious freedom has rarely been tolerated in the world's history, for it signifies the limiting of political power by pointing to a higher authority to which it is accountable.

Idolatry in the Old Testament takes two forms: it may be either a commitment to false gods or the construction of false images of the true God (the two are prohibited in the first two commandments of the Law – Ex 24:3–4). On the one hand, human beings are prone to substitute their own ideas, value systems or structures for God, and then seek God's blessing upon their creations. On the other hand, they often worship a god apparently tolerant of injustice and the oppressive use of power, more concerned with stability, order and continuity in society than with its transformation. Idolatry is the blatant or subtle manipulation of God for personal or community ends. For this reason some believe that it is more serious than atheism. Such a suggestion might be true, were it not for the fact that human nature abhors a spiritual and moral vacuum. Atheism, therefore (as in the communist system), can quickly lead to an alternative 'theism' (an ideal which demands absolute belief and commitment).

The problem of idolatry is that it leads human beings away from seeking and trusting the liberating God. It is an escape into false securities, illusions ('peace, peace where there is no peace'), false alliances and wrong commitments. In each of these instances politics can be idolatrous. In reality it often is. Political life becomes specifically idolatrous either when a nation looks for its security in its military superiority to (or at least parity with) other nations (Is 30:1–15; 31:1–3; Ezek 17:15–18) or when it makes the creation and enjoyment of wealth an end in itself (Eph 5:5; Col 3:5; Mt 6:24). In these latter passages idolatry is equated with greed – a deliberate submission to the power that comes from possessing money, and a belief that it is legitimate to satisfy ever-expanding wants.

(e) God and the nations

Another facet of idolatry in the Old Testament is the tribalism which creates a god to protect the interests of a particular ethnic group. The liberating God of Abraham and of the Exodus, who gives the Law, warns against centralised political power and castigates idolatrous political philosophies and practices is anything but a tribal god. He frequently judges the nation he has chosen to fulfil his purposes and has mercy on those who do not know either his liberating power or his Law (Nineveh is the supreme example).

God is international in his activities. He is the God who holds the nations in the hollow of his hand and orders their doings and relationships. Though the Old Testament writers are primarily interested in the other nations because of their relationship to Israel, they speak of a God who is concerned about them in their own right. A significant feature of the prophets are the oracles of judgement upon the nations. Beginning with Amos, God shows himself consistently scandalised by the actions of nations who carry on their politics by acts of excessive cruelty and violence. He judges them according to the general moral consciousness which they possess: loyalty to treaties (Amos 1:9); the claims of mercy (1:11); the protection of women, especially those who are pregnant (1:13); the sanctity of the dead (2:2). Their own innate sense of right and wrong is the equivalent of the Law of the Lord (Amos 2:4; Rom 2:14–15) until such time as they learn for themselves the content of that Law (Is 2:3; 51:4; Zech 8:20–23).

God expects all the nations to respond to the moral sensibility they possess. They, and not only Israel, will be held accountable for the actions they take. Nations may repent of their wickedness and seek the Lord's favour. For God is compassionate upon them, as he is upon his own special people (Jon 4:11). He even enacts a covenant with them and calls them his people (Is 19:25), promising that he will heal and bless them (Is 19:22). The Egyptians, like the Israelites who suffered at their hands centuries before, will cry to the Lord because of their suffering. God will hear their cry, send them a deliverer, liberate them and teach them true worship of himself (Is 19:19ff).

God, then, is constantly active in the life of the nations. International relations are under his control, and the ebb and flow of war and peace are made to serve his ends. Indeed, it is part of the prophetic task to discern the signs of the times by interpreting the politics of the day as instances of God's judgement and mercy at work. Assyria and Babylon were used as instruments of God's anger against his special people. They soon discovered, however, that they were not exempt from judgement and were punished for their arrogant and ruthless use of power. Cyrus the Mede was also an instrument of God's mercy to his people in restoring them to their land (Is 44:28; 45:1; 61:5–9).

Jeremiah, in particular, was given the task of telling his people how the international events of the day revealed God's secret workings. He had the unpalatable task of informing them that God had called for the conquest of their land by a foreign power. As a consequence, it was futile for them either to fight, seek military alliances or try to escape to neighbouring nations (Jer 27; 42:18–43:7; Is 36:9). The sanctity of nationhood was not inviolate. If a nation would not hear the voice of God (and the prophets had an international ministry – cf Jer 27:3ff), then its political life might be suspended for a time by invasion and deportation. The suffering they received was the direct outcome of idolatry (Amos 2:7–8). A nation may be at greatest risk when it believes itself to be secure, just in its policies and enjoying God's favour.

(f) Peace with justice

These two great Old Testament themes are on the lips of millions today.

Peace (*shalom*) has a broad meaning in the Old Testament. In this it differs from common modern usage. Whereas normally we think of peace from a negative point of view (the absence of conflict and violence), the Old Testament understands it in positive terms. The root meaning of *shalom* is 'completeness' or 'wholeness'. It is fulness of life on earth in God's presence.

This fulness has four main strands to it:

(i)   Material well-being for the entire community (Job 15:21; Pss 37:11; 72:7; 122:6);

(ii)   Health (Ps 38:3; Is 38:16–17);

(iii   Security from both actual and potential threats of enemies (Job 5:24);

(iv)   A life of fellowship and partnership with God, when he has no cause to rebuke or judge (Is 53:5; 54:10; Jer 29:11; Mk 2:6).

Peace in biblical thinking is not an isolated concept. It cannot be possessed by itself and for itself. A number of conditions have to be fulfilled, the main one being the presence of justice. A constant refrain of the prophets is that 'there is no peace for the wicked' (Is 57:21; 48:22). Where justice is absent *shalom* is impossible – 'the way of peace they know not and there is no justice in their paths' (Is 59:8, RSV). Peace can come only when the Lord's controversy against 'swearing, lying, killing, stealing and committing adultery' (Hos 4:1–3) has ended. So peace is an illusory goal until people learn 'to do what is just, to show constant love, and to live in humble fellowship with our God' (Mic 6:8). Those who proclaim peace in the midst of a situation where conflict abounds because of unresolved injustices, unrighteous practices and the neglect of God are false prophets, perverting the cause of truth.

Justice is one of the basic characteristics of God. There is no independent, universal, ideal definition of justice by which to understand God's justice, for he alone is the source of its meaning. Justice in the Bible is not an abstract concept nor some heavenly ideal. First and foremost it is how God acts.

We know God's justice by his acts of deliverance and by the laws he has given.

At the risk of over-simplification, five basic aspects of justice seem to stand out in the Bible (I expand the significance of each one of these further on page 119f.).

First, *justice is the impartial upholding of the Law*. Those responsible for administrating the Law must always make true judgements (Ps 72:1–2; Prov 29:4). Therefore, justice is perverted when bribes are offered and threats are made (Deut 16:19–20), when it is not available to the whole population (Ex 18:13–26) and when it is delayed (Lev 19:15).

Secondly, *it is the right use of power*. Authorities are to use their office to establish an environment of truthfulness and rectitude in the whole nation.

Thirdly, *it is the defence of the poor*. It is exercised by standing alongside powerless people, being their advocate and delivering them (Prov 31:8–9). Partiality is to be shown to the unprotected (Ps 146:6–7).

Fourthly, *it is the salvation of the ungodly*. God's salvation is accomplished when God upholds his justice, and yet at the same time forgives the unjust person and creates in him or her a new desire to do right (Is 45:21; 45:8; 46:13; Rom 3:25–26). Salvation is the coming together of love and justice. Love does not forgive in spite of injustice, and yet justice does not condemn and exact full and final retribution against the claims of love. Justice is both prior to and yet subservient to love. Love is shaped by justice and makes it work in concrete and personal ways.

Fifthly, *it is a life of complete personal integrity*, brought about through the pursuit of a deliberate policy of total honesty. In particular, justice is incompatible with the misrepresentation of others (Tit 2:11).

Justice, then, is the way into peace. Exhortations in the Old Testament to act justly are directed usually to the political leaders of the day. In the political sphere this is God's foremost requirement.

(g) Political life recreated

Peace and justice are the main characteristics of a new age which God's anointed servant will inaugurate (Is 9:6–7). He is to be a ruler completely after God's heart, who will accomplish everything that the monarchs in Israel failed to do.

The clearest picture of life in this 'new age' comes in Micah 4:1–4 (Is 2:2–4) and Isaiah 65:17–25. All causes of sorrow and distress will be removed from the community. People will be healthy and strong (Is 65:20). They will fully enjoy the fruit of their own labour, for the full value of their work will accrue to them, rather than to others (Is 65:22). The original harmony between human beings will be restored (Is 65:23), bringing with it the end of nature's being 'red in tooth and claw' (Is 65:25). Harmony between people and God will also be restored (Is 65:23–24). War will no longer be 'the pursuit of diplomacy by other means' (Mic 4:3). And, finally, everyone will be able equally to enjoy God's rich Creation without fear that some, out of greed, will try to accumulate to themselves more than their share (Mic 4:4).

This community of peace and justice is promised as the destiny of the world. The utopian vision is not, however, a simple continuation of the present world order. Rather, the idolatry and injustice of our present way of life (death) will first be judged and terminated before a new way of being human can be reconstructed according to God's blueprint.

From a biblical perspective the new order cannot be a secular society, for this is but the latest kind in a long line of societies alienated from the true and living God. The new earth will operate according to the principle the French Catholic philospher, Jacques Maritain, called 'theocratic humanism' – an unselfish concern for others springing from a life centred on God, whose love will have penetrated all human relationships.

The new order cannot be pluralist either, in the sense that conflicts between rival claims to truth remain unresolved. In the new age we will all know fully and practice completely the one truth whose source is God. All political life in the new world will be done as an offering of worship to God and as a service to one's neighbour.

2 The New Testament

(a) How the two Testaments relate to each other

Many of the difficulties associated with applying the Bible to political life spring from questions about the relationship between the two Testaments. What degree of continuity is there between Israel's Bible and the documents written by Jesus' apostles or their close associates? Can we read the Old Testament by itself, discovering there a coherent message that stands on its own without immediate reference to the New Testament? Or should a Christian only interpret the Old Testament after absorbing the account of Jesus of Nazareth?

These are not academic quibbles. How we understand the meaning the New Testament writers gave to some of the great concepts of the Old Testament like peace, justice and the kingdom depends entirely on our answer to these questions. When, for example, Paul states that Jesus Christ 'is our peace' (Eph 2:14), how much of the Old Testament notion of *shalom* is contained in his thoughts? And how much does the phrase contain a new depth of meaning derived from the fact that Jesus Christ has fulfilled all God's promises?

Answers to these questions are vitally important. On the surface at least, the New Testament does not appear to engage so directly with political life as the Old Testament. However, if in understanding God's purpose we can detect a strong continuity between the two, then this judgement may be superficial. Once we accept that silence in the New Testament does not demonstrate disinterest, but is the result of a continuity with the Old which does not have to be repeated at every point, we can affirm that the New Testament may be just as overtly political as the Old.

Nevertheless, there are differences between the two Testaments. Two main ones stand out. First, and obviously, the historical context has changed. With John the Baptist prophecy comes back on the scene again. Jesus and his disciples carry it on. However, God's Word is given through them in circumstances substantially changed from Old Testament times. As well as being related to former prophecy, it is also set firmly against the social, political and religious realities of the Mediterranean world of the first century.

Secondly, much of the New Testament is born out of controversy with the Jews as to how the Old Testament should be interpreted and applied to the new situation. The early Christians did not so much claim a wholly new understanding of Scripture as a return to its essential meaning, over against the various distortions prevalent amongst Jewish groups of the time. In this sense they claimed to be the true heirs of the Law, the prophets and the writings. Naturally, the coming of Jesus produced a way of handling the Old Testament which brought out its deeper meaning, particularly in the generally recognised messianic passages.

However we evaluate the change which took place from one Testament to the other, most interpreters would agree that two major aspects of God's purposes come into clearer focus in the New Testament.

First, *the appearance of the Messiah brings a crisis into the heart of the Israelite nation.* Jesus' call to faith and discipleship provokes a division among the people. From now on, inevitably, two communities exist side by side. Paul gives extended theological consideration to the reasons for the division (Rom chapters 9–11). He concludes that the reality of division within the Hebrew people is not new. Rather, Christ's presence brings it into sharper relief.

God has always based his relationship with his people on his calling (election) and not on ethnic identity. They are bound to him, therefore, by faith and obedience, and not by fulfilling the ritual and cultural requirements of nationhood (the works of the Law). The choice between the two brought a separation of Jew from Jew (Lk 17:33–35). Paul then develops his theological explanation of what has happened round the idea of the remnant (Rom 2:28–29; 9:6–8).

Secondly, *God's people are no longer identified with one nation.*
The incorporation of Greeks, barbarians and Scythians into
the community of God's people (Col 3:11) was hard for the
early Christian Jews to accept. The apostolic leadership of
the new community of the Messiah came to accept that this
was God's plan, though not without misgivings in high places.
According to the promise to Abraham (Gen 12:2), the implications of God's calling and grace and the prophetic message
about 'the day of the Lord', all peoples are included in
God's provision of salvation. The reality of a transnational,
corporate body committed to Jesus Christ has profound
implications for understanding the political relevance of the
gospel, though the Church has often been slow to grasp this.

(b) The supreme authority

The story and message of the New Testament centre on
Jesus and the kingdom (cf Acts 1:3; 8:12; 19:8; 28:23; 31).
Both the Church and political life in the State, in different
ways, derive their meaning and functions from these two
events.

Jesus' public ministry was worked out in line with his
declaration that God's kingdom of justice and peace had
broken into the daily reality of people and nations. He
demonstrated its power at work in nature, personal relationships and in religious and political life.[1]

Jesus' call to discipleship ('follow me') is, therefore, a call
to 'seek first the kingdom and its justice (Mt 6:33), 'to enter
the kingdom' (Mk 10:15; Jn 3:5) and 'to take the yoke of the
kingdom' upon one (Mt 11:29–30). God's people are invited
and challenged to orientate their whole lives round the
kingdom.

The one who issues the call, however, is not like any other
religious or political leader. He is greater than Solomon
the king and Jonah the prophet (Mt 12:41–42). The post-
Resurrection confession, 'my Lord and my God' (Jn 20:28)
is an indispensable foundation for all New Testament belief.
Jesus of Nazareth is king of the Jews (Jn 19:19–20), and of
the Romans too (19:5,11).

Authority in the public life of communities is, therefore, a relative, derived and accountable exercise of power. Lords and deities of all kinds are subjected to the one supreme Lord over all (1 Cor 8:5–6). Within this relationship, however, civil authorities have divinely granted functions and responsibilities.

(c) The governing authorities

Paul makes this point about civil authorities in the famous and much disputed passage, Romans 13:1–7. Much has and will continue to be written about these verses. I will return to the passage again in Chapter 8, giving it more attention there. For the moment, within our present limited purpose of identifying the relevant biblical material, the following points seem worth considering.

(i) According to the immediate context (Rom 12:17–21), the Christians in Rome were apparently tempted to take the Law into their own hands and apply the principle of retribution against their persecutors (Rom 12:14,19). They may have come to the conclusion that such action was a legitimate deduction from their freedom in Christ (Rom 13:12). Paul tells them that this is not so, for God has arranged life in society differently.

(ii) The State authorities were responsible for carrying out the work of 'repaying back evil for evil' (Rom 12:17,19) by bringing 'God's punishment on those who do evil' (Rom 13:4; compare Rom 12:19 – 'I will pay back, says the Lord'). In this instance we may presume that the wrongdoing was being committed both by some people persecuting Christians and by some Christians retaliating in kind. The State's responsibility is to maintain peace and harmony within a society always likely to break apart into factions. It does this both by rigorously controlling evil and by rewarding deeds of goodness (Rom 13:3–4).

(iii) Paul has in mind here the state *faithfully* fulfilling its God-appointed tasks. Its work is defined and circumscribed by the good (i.e. God's absolute demand for justice), not by its own laws. When Paul writes (Rom 13:1), 'for no authority exists without God's permission', he is saying more than that God has established actual, particular governments. He implies that no political authority is ever self-established and self-authenticating. Its authority does not come from itself, nor (by deduction) does it receive it from the people who may elect it to power.

(iv) Two main consequences flow from the fact that God through Jesus Christ is sovereign over all the powers. First, governments are God's servants in so far as 'they fulfil their duties' (Rom 13:6), by administrating justice and punishing evil. They cease to be God's agents as soon as they compromise over justice and injustice. Secondly, all citizens (including Christians) are to submit to the reality of political authority. *Submission* does not however, imply that they should *obey* (Paul uses a different word for the two ideas) every injuction of every individual state. Indeed, some commentators on this passage suggest that disobedience to certain laws which enforce unjust policies is a real form of submission in that it demonstrates a serious concern for the integrity of the state.[2]

(v) Probably the famous phrase of Christ concerning the payment of tax, 'pay the Emperor what belongs to the Emperor, and pay to God what belongs to God', is intended to convey that the State has a limited function to receive taxes in order to carry out its legitimate work (Rom 13:7). In this sense we are to submit to it, but never to serve it, for divine service belongs only to God.

(d) Demonic authorities

There is a strong tradition in the New Testament (particularly in the book of Revelation) which sets the State in the context of idolatry and even demonology. The State may not find it convenient to distinguish between submission and service. It is constantly tempted to turn itself into an object of reverence, and demand an allegiance beyond its legitimate right. By failing to recognise and acknowledge its authority as derived, subordinate and 'secular', it ascribes to itself a quasi-religious value. The picture of Rome in Revelation is one with Pharoah's Egypt, with Assyria, Babylon and numerous states in the twentieth century.

Most states of the ancient world encouraged a distinction between public religion (a formality in which one paid one's respect to the king's divine nature as the representative of the gods) and private belief (a matter of individual choice, about which the State remained indifferent).

Many modern states continue the tradition in the form either of an established church (one of whose function is to legitimise publicly the symbols of State authority) or of a totally secular government (in which religion is debarred altogether from interfering with the practice of power).

The early Church, however, could not make the distinction between the public and the private. Their 'private' belief that Jesus was Lord of all, to whom all authority in heaven and earth had been entrusted, and to whom all God's enemies would be subjected, had 'public' implications.

The demand was, and remains, that the State be non-religious in the sense of refraining from trying to manipulate religious symbols or institutions for its own benefit, and yet that it be held 'religiously' accountable to the one Lord over all.

The failure of the early Church to submit to the requirements of the State religion brought it into direct confrontation with the governing authorities. As a result it suffered persecution. Out of persecution was developed a theory of the perversion of State authority which in Paul's letters took the form of 'the principalities and powers' (cf 1 Cor 2:8; Acts 13:27, Eph 6:12; Col 1:16), and in Revelation that of 'the dragon and the beast' (chapters 12, 13).[3]

3 Conclusion

The State is instituted by God to be an instrument of his justice. It is given the necessary space to fulfil its task. However, it may easily abuse its responsibility and freedom and slide into idolatrous claims and demands. When it does so, citizens of all kinds, and the Christian Church in particular, are bound to resist its absolute claims for itself or any of its policies. When circumstances demand, the resistance may be considered part of a genuine submission, to the end that the State may again be what God constituted.

The Church's particular nature and calling may make it into a focal point of criticism against the government (often in totalitarian states the only one), whenever the latter abandons its God-given role.

The Church is no longer itself a nation or an ethnically homogeneous people. Rather, it is made up of many nationalities. Its calling to follow Jesus Christ (to many political authorities a scandal) sets it apart from the main political preoccupations of power, stability and continuity. Being the community of the king, its main task is to bear witness in word and deed to both the reality and demands of Christ's rule.

The main political consequence of the separation of Church and State, following the coming of Christ, is the establishment of an organised critical body within the political life of nations. One of its major tasks is to monitor the extent to which justice is being implemented within and between identifiable political jurisdictions. In order to do this work effectively and impartially the Church must keep itself free of entanglement with detailed political processes.

Notes

1   Cf A Kirk, *A New World Coming* (Basingstoke, Marshalls, 1983) Chap 4.

2   There can be no infallible guide to what is just and unjust, unless the action in question is unmistakenly commended or condemned by God's written Word. Every person must make up their mind, seeking to be guided by a conscience grounded in God's revealed will and free from prejudice and vested interest.

3   In Chapter 8 we will return to a more extended treatment of this theme.

VI

Building Bridges

When we want to apply the Bible in specific ways, it is easy to see the problems. To arrive at convincing conclusions is much more difficult. In bringing the Bible to bear on modern issues we are trying to answer two questions. First, if the text originally specified a particular course of action, what action should I (we) take as a consequence? For example, both Paul and Peter told Christians 'to submit yourselves for the Lord's sake to every authority ... whether to the king ... or to governors' (1 Pet 2:13–14; Rom 13 1ff). How should I (we) respond today to that command given 2,000 years ago? Secondly, how do I discover in the Bible guidelines or norms which will cause me to choose one course of action rather than another? To put the matter slightly differently, how may I use the Bible to find the mind of Christ (1 Cor 2:16; 2 Cor 10:5) in a particular situation which confronts me? How may I be God's instrument to be part of the answer to the prayer, 'Your will be done on earth as it is in heaven'? These questions help to define the main purpose of reading and interpreting the Bible: *to understand how God's Word, given specifically and uniquely at one point of time, becomes God's Word to us today in such a way as to demand obedience.*

For reasons we have already discussed, the application of Bible texts cannot be mechanical. There may be some occasions when a command can be obeyed literally, exactly as it was originally given. We should not automatically discount such a possibility for fear of a wooden, unthinking literalism. We should also beware of using the problems sometimes associated with application as an excuse for not taking biblical teaching at its face value. A general command like 'do not lie to each other' (Col 3:9) is valid at all times and in all places. Its observation would have a revolutionary effect on political life. However, even here it is possible to think of extreme situations, like giving false information to an intending murderer to protect a potential victim, or to an enemy to thwart aggressive intentions, where the universal command has to be suspended.

Application involves building bridges between two historical situations, both of which are vitally important for hearing and understanding God's Word. One of the major assumptions Christians make about their faith is that God continues to make effective the salvation from sin which Christ's death and resurrection has made possible for all people in all situations for all time. We are part of the same history of salvation as the early Church and living proof of its reality. We interpret the Bible, therefore, in the context of the way in which God's salvation in Christ is becoming real to us. What this means is that we have to find out how God speaks today on the basis of how he spoke in biblical times.

There are two kinds of errors to avoid in this bridge-building process. First, if we want to hear God's Word to us, and not just an echo of our own voice, we cannot allow modern beliefs to be the norm for measuring the text's meaning. As one person has graphically put it, for some people, whatever the net of modern thinking does not catch is not a fish! This is arrogant self-sufficiency. It assumes that we have an independent source of truth about reality which is able to give a final verdict on claims to truth coming from the past. The Christian view of life rejects the notion that there are eternal truths accessible to us independently of Jesus of Nazareth – God in human form. Moreover, the idea that we can accept from the Bible only what the modern mind finds to its liking would mean imposing on the Bible wholly alien categories. The Bible would cease to be a critical point of reference. Its truth would be made dependent on our decision to assent to it or turn it down.

Secondly, we must be very careful not to fall into the trap of slavish imitation. There are some Christians who would like to be able to reproduce exactly the political, economic and family life of ancient Israel or the structures of the New Testament Church. However, as has been pointed out, this approach reduces God to 'once upon a time'. He would be a God who acted and spoke once centuries ago but who has long since dropped into a deep sleep. It denies the importance of every moment of history as the time when God continues to offer us forgiveness and spur us to collaborate with him in transforming the world. We live between the moment when God first specifically promised his people that he would create a new heaven and a new earth and the realisation of what he said. But our moment of history will be already a partial fulfilment of that promise, if God is who he says he is. We interpret the Bible in part, then, to discern the signs of God's promise coming true.

So, each moment of history has to be taken seriously and given its due weight. That being said, we still need to ask exactly how we may know what the Bible tells us to do as Christ's disciples in our generation. Interpreters of the Bible have used a number of different words to try to express practical ways of building bridges. We might call them a convoy of vehicles moving back and forth across the bridge, each one with its own capacity to do the job of conveying the necessary knowledge from one side to the other. None of them are perfect. If we were going to do a consumer report on each we would find they all had both strong and weak points. We do not necessarily see them as competing goods on offer. Rather, by using all of them in the right way we can do a more effective job of transportation.

1 The model

A model is a plan or a design. It is a representation (like a scaled-down model of a school or hospital) which is to be followed in construction. It is a pattern to be copied. In this sense some have seen events and institutions in the life of Israel as models for us to follow. A good example (as a model of a decentralised form of government) might be the Confederation of Tribes at the time of the Judges. Or, conversely, the advent of a king in Israel might be an anti-model – that is, a warning against a centralised and hereditary dynasty (cf Judg 8:22–23).

The Confederation of Tribes is said to represent a perfect balance between centralised and dispersed power. Each tribe was semi-autonomous within its own jurisdiction, and yet was bound to all the others, establishing a certain national unity, by the solemn ratification of a pact (Josh chapter 24). When occasion demanded, they acted together either to deal with a particularly grave crime within one tribe (Judg chapters 19–20) or to protect their territorial integrity from invasion. However, there was probably no permanent co-ordinating authority, like a council of tribal representatives, and no leader of the stature of Moses or Joshua.

Whether this rather unstructured way of being a nation was considered a model in later Israel is difficult to answer. Certainly, after four-and-a-half centuries of more centralised government under a monarchy, Israel returned after the Exile to a pattern resembling that of the Confederation. They would have asked themselves the question, 'Which pattern of political authority best represents the ideal of a theocracy?'

The advantage of using events in the Bible as models to be copied is that it delivers us from vague generalisations and abstract principles. These latter are in danger of being so inadequately defined that they are not much concrete use. Moreover, some would argue that God uses models, rather than principles, in order to show the practical application in human society of his revealed will (cf 2 Tim 1:13).

However, the discovery of models does not answer all the problems of application. In particular, it is necessary to find out whether the institution in question was intended to be a universal model, or one particularly suited to a given historical situation. If the model is judged to possess a timeless relevance, we still have to ask how it can be transposed to a different situation. For example, do all parts of a model have to be valid, or equally applicable? Can we, over a period of time, re-design aspects of the model (e.g. the size of the computer room in a new school complex) to take care of changing circumstances?

Another advantage of the model is that it does not allow us to escape easily from concrete and often difficult questions, such as an economic system in which interest is not charged (the Islamic banking system is an attempt to apply a model along these lines). The model controls the search for general principles of application. And yet to discover God's social design for today does involve transferring laws and institutions across time and cultures. An exact reproduction of a model, even if it were practicably feasible, would ignore historical development. The Federation of Cantons in Switzerland might be the nearest modern example of the Confederation of Tribes in Israel. It can only work, however, if there is a more structured process of consultation and decision-making, which all the separate states agree to be bound by, than existed after the death of Joshua in Israel.

2 Middle axioms

The direct application of the Confederation model to Britain would be difficult because there is little sense of corporate belonging on a regional basis (except in Wales, Scotland and Northern Ireland). If it has a relevance, it has to be found in another way. The use of middle axioms might be one.

A middle axiom is a specific principle which stands either between a universal proposition and a concrete situation or between concrete applications in different situations. In the first case, we could affirm that the defence and propagation of human rights is a self-evident, universal, moral obligation. However, because the Bible does not use the language of rights as such, in order to apply relevant biblical categories to the actual world of human rights we need to find intermediate principles. Following this example, such principles might be the

meaning of being human and the meaning of justice. In the
second case, we have to extract from one concrete situation
(e.g. the Confederation of Tribes) the appropriate principles
which correspond to a different concrete reality. In other
words, the middle axiom is the intention which can be found
behind the concrete historical form.

In the case of Britain, the middle axiom might be the
decentralisation of political power, leading to regional
autonomy and the consequent increase of the decision-
making authority of local government. In the application of
middle axioms one would then have to ask further specific
questions about institutions such as Metropolitan authorities
and policies such as rate-capping (the limiting of funds from
central government to local authorities which charge too
much local tax). If we work backwards from current issues
to the biblical text does the middle axiom help us to clarify
the intention behind the particular laws and institutions of
Israel?

Naturally, the discovery and use of middle axioms does
not solve every problem. There is the difficulty, for example,
of deciding which middle axiom should be derived from the
biblical situation. In the case of offering the other cheek to
one who is evil, what intermediate principle do we suggest?
Some would say it is the absolute physical integrity of all
human beings, implying total pacifism. Others would say it
is the law of non-retaliation applied to purely *personal* griev-
ances, implying that the restraint of violence by physical
means against *third* parties is perfectly legitimate. The
problem of the first deduction is how to apply the command
not to resist evil in a social context without promoting
anarchy. The problem of the second deduction is how to
distinguish a Christian's response to violence in society from
any other and how to relate it specifically to the action which
Jesus himself took in a violent situation.

A similar difficulty relates to apparent conflicts of principles. From studying Israel and the early Church's attitudes
to the creation, ownership and use of wealth, a number of
middle axioms might be deduced: the 'State' did not own

property, for ownership was invested in the family and the clan; in the face of poverty every Israelite was to care for their neighbour (the principle of redistribution); the accumulation of wealth for purely personal ends is seen as idolatry (the serving of Mammon); all individuals are personally accountable to God for the use they make of God's physical resources and their own talents. All of these statements are irrefutably derived directly from the text. The problem is that some point in the direction of a 'socialist' society, built on the prime need to redistribute wealth, whilst others point to the 'capitalist' virtues of freedom from State control and individual initiative.

In the face of the conflict, some Christians have chosen one set of middle axioms rather than another. Others have tried to devise a society in which the strengths of each are incorporated – progressive taxation; co-operative ownership; the State as a minimal owner. Whilst others claim that Israelite economic reality already presents in model form a harmonisation of principles.

3 Dynamic equivalents

Because of the relative difficulties in using either models or middle axioms as effective means of transferring relevant information across the bridge in order to find the mind of Christ, some Christians have turned to a concept which has come into fashion in recent times.

Dynamic equivalents is an idea borrowed from the work of translating one language into another. The intention is to convey to contemporary readers, using appropriate forms, meanings *equivalent* to those understood by the original readers. It is contrasted as a method with 'formal correspondence', whose main concern is to imitate by translating literally word for word.

A dynamic equivalent works on the basis of being able to distinguish between form and content. In searching for God's revealed will, the content remains the same across the ages. The outward form, however, may change dramatically both in terms of social development from simple to complex societies and of culture, from what is appropriate in one community's set of traditions to another. Obviously, in the process of applying the Bible it is important to safeguard the essential content of the original pattern, so that one can say with confidence that this form today *corresponds* to the purpose behind that institution yesterday.

Following this type of 'transport', some have suggested that the equivalent of owning land in an agricultural community might be that of owning a house, or a small business, in an urban, industrial society. The equivalent of the remission of debts in the Jubilee year legislation (Lev 25:25–28) might be the scaling down of interest rates according to a person's, company's or nation's ability to repay. The purpose behind the legislation would be understood as a means of counteracting a situation of perpetual impoverishment (as is the case of many individual debtors and debtor nations today). Greater flexibility over debt might save some businesses from having to go into liquidation with the subsequent human tragedy of extensive loss of jobs.

The dynamic equivalent to the principle of subordination to political authorities (Rom 13:1ff; 1 Pet 2:13–14) would depend on the political circumstances of each nation. If one took a model approach, following the exact practice of the early Church, subordination would mean political non-involvement and obedience to all laws and institutions of the State (with the one exception of the cult to the Emperor). Even in this case one would be alert to the modern equivalents of the exception: perhaps the prohibition in some countries to teach one's children the faith of Jesus Christ.

A dynamic equivalent approach, on the other hand, would allow both active co-operation and further reasons for resisting the demands of the State. Hence, in totalitarian states which both pay lip service to and yet suppress human rights, Christians would interpret subordination not as passive inaction but as active opposition to the flouting of God's purposes for political authority.

It could be argued that the purpose (or *middle axiom*)

behind slavery, as an institution allowed by the Bible, was to protect the weaker members of society against exploitation in a decentralised economy. One needs to remember that the Biblical *model* of slavery was vastly different from that of surrounding nations. The *dynamic equivalent* today might be found in the provision of social security for the unemployed, laws governing minimum wages and unfair dismissal and in practices like fostering children at risk.

4 Deduction

Whichever of the previous methods of transport we use to carry relevant material across the bridge from one situation to another, we are bound to reinterpret the text as soon as we try to apply its message.

Specific guidance and direction can only be made by a process of deduction. Sometimes this may be a laborious process of moving slowly and deliberately from one stage in an argument to another. At other times it may happen as a flash of inspiration, an intuitive grasp of the way different parts of a jig-saw fit together to complete the picture.

Once we have seen that an automatic, unthinking application of any part of Scripture is impossible, we acknowledge that a process of re-application must go on. This may take one of a number of different forms. For example, we may seek to identify *a general claim* behind a specific moral judgement – such as 'you shall not remove your neighbour's landmark' (Deut 19:14; 27:17), or, 'when a man is newly married, he shall not go out with the army or be charged with any business; he shall be free at home one year, to be happy with his wife whom he has taken' (24:5) – and then deduce an equivalent practice for changed circumstances.

Alternatively, we may look at interpretation from the point of view of the political concerns which face us today and ask ourselves, what are the *precedents* which occurred in biblical times? A precedent is a judicial decision which serves as an authority in deciding later legal cases. Or, it is an example which is used to justify similar events later on. The idea fits well into the idea of case law, in which a lawyer will argue by analogy from one case to another.

Clearly, to use the biblical material as precedent we have to establish the nature and degree of correspondence between divergent situations. The interpreter asks the question, if in those given circumstances that course of action was taken, what course is demanded or suggested in these similar circumstances.

As an example, we might take the State's encroachment on individual civil liberties: for example, its demand to have extensive information on all its citizens; its right, even in peace-time, to draft each male citizen into the armed forces for obligatory military service; its claim to have the right to curtail freedom of movement by granting or withholding passports and to declare states of emergency with the provision of holding people incommunicado for lengthy periods of time, without charges being laid against them. What are the biblical precedents which would help us to decide how to react to all these common practices of actual modern states? Precedents for military service might be the progressive reduction of Gideon's army (Judg 7:2ff) and the valid reasons for not joining the army announced in Deuteronomy 20:5–8. At the same time, the call to arms in times of national distress suggests a conscript army (cf 2 Chron 17:14; 25:5; Num 26:2), whilst a small professional army was begun by Saul and carried on by David and some of his successors (1 Sam 14:52; 22:2; 2 Chron 11:11–12). The conversion of Roman soldiers in the New Testament might also seem to provide precedents. However, their situation is ambiguous, as we do not know what attitude to their profession they took subsequent to becoming Christians.

In the case of the other examples of encroachment on freedom, it is difficult to imagine the existence of precedents in a society where the kind of sophisticated control and surveillance practised by modern states was impossible. A negative precedent to the practice of long detention without trial might be the total absence in Israel of punishment by imprisonment and the demand that legal judgements be made swiftly. However, temporary custody until a judgement was made is known in two cases, Lev 24:12 and Num 15:34, and arbitrary arrest and detention in two others, 1 Kings 22:27; Jer 37:15–18.

5 Conclusion

We have tried to set out, with relevant examples, some of the possible ways in which the text of Scripture may be brought alongside contemporary reality in order that we may hear God's Word speaking to us. None of the methods produce fool-proof, clear-cut and wholly unambiguous answers to questions of practice. Each needs to be tried and tested, using other examples and issues than the ones I have suggested here. The usefulness of the method will then be shown in the course of actually employing it.

VII

Applying The Old Testament

The purpose of this and the following chapter is to illustrate a method. The idea is to take three aspects of the Old and New Testaments and relate them as closely as is possible to the political life of the late twentieth century. The selection is personal, many other themes and passages could have been chosen. However, the point is not to try to discuss all the possible political implications of the whole Old or New Testament, but to take a few examples to show how the text might be used. The reader may like to reflect, bearing in mind the discussion of the last chapter, which of the examples of transportation across the bridge are applicable to the different pieces of material which are discussed in these two chapters.

I have chosen one institution (the monarchy), one book (Micah) and one theme (justice). In the first and last case we will continue the discussion we began in Chapters 2 and 5.

1 The monarchy

Kings existed in Israel for a relatively short time in comparison to the nation's entire history from the time of Abraham to (say) the coming of the Romans in 63 BC. The span from Saul to Jehoiachim and Zedekiah was about four-and-a-half centuries. It was an eventful time. The nation expanded its territory and developed its economy under

David and Solomon, only to split up into two nations under Rehoboam and Jeroboam.

Judging by the comments passed on most kings by Israel's historians and the twin disasters of exile to Assyria and Babylon, government by monarchy was not a great success. There were some notable exceptions – David, Hezekiah, Josiah and Uzziah. They proved the rule.

The monarchy arose in confused circumstances. Israel was being threatened by the Philistines, a force far more powerful than any they had had to face at the time of the judges. Saul appears at first as one who continues the judges' work. He is chosen and sent by God, in response to the people's cries of anguish, to deliver them from the danger that their national life would disintegrate (1 Sam 9:16; 10:1–2). However, unlike the Judges, he did not return to his former occupation after delivering Jabesh-Gilead from the Ammonites (1 Sam 11:1ff; 12:2). Rather, the whole people demanded that Saul be made king (1 Sam 8:5; 10:19; 11:15; 12:12). As was not the case with Gideon (Judg 7:22–23), this was accepted. In practice this meant that Saul was the commander-in-chief of a standing army and was occupied for most of his reign with keeping the Philistines at bay. Centralisation and control of all the tribes began to take place more effectively under David.

Saul's becoming king clearly marked a new departure for Israel. God allowed the request, though without approving it. Through Samuel he made it clear that the request signified a form of apostasy (1 Sam 10:17–19). To have a permanent institution of kingship signalled a failure to trust God to raise up the necessary leaders in times of crisis (1 Sam 12:11). It meant, therefore, that the people were beginning to put their trust in the institution as a means of security. In this way they showed themselves no different from other nations, who made no pretence of believing in and following the living God (1 Sam 8:5).

Samuel rebuked them not only for unbelief, but for failing to see the political consequences of their folly. Having a permanent king brought negative repercussions to the life of the nation.

David's reign was different in kind from that of Saul. He became king over Israel as well as the powerful tribes of Judah and Benjamin (2 Sam 2:4; 5:1–5), and even in times of relative peace he maintained a standing army (or national guard – 2 Sam 5:6f; 5:21; 21:15). These professional troops remained a separate body, distinct from the conscripted army recruited in a time of emergency (2 Sam 11:1). They included mercenaries (the Cherethites and Pelethites – 2 Sam 8:18; 15:18; 20:7). They were exempted from taxes and forced labour (1 Sam 17:25), and granted lands or a claim on tithes (1 Sam 8:14–15).

Moreover, David not only brought about a national unity under his personal leadership, but he began to create an empire. Non-Israelite populations like the Philistines, Edomites, Ammonites, Moabites and Aramaeans were brought into his kingdom by conquest (2 Sam 8:1–14). Sometimes their own kings were allowed to reign as vassals, sometimes David installed his own governors over them. Perhaps David was aspiring to fill the power vacuum left by the decline of Egypt. The idea of empire persisted under Solomon (1 Kings 4:24; 9:19), though part of it was lost during his reign (1 Kings 11:14–25).

So, one of the major effects of monarchy was the building up of military power and the territorial expansion of the nation, which required yet more troops. Apart from anything else, the expanding army had to be supported. This was a financial burden on the nation. It was paid for by raising a levy (or taxation) on the produce of the land and on livestock, or by simply taking property belonging to a family or clan (1 Sam 8:14; 1 Kings 21:7; Ezek 46:18).

Another effect was that of forced labour. Israel was subject to it in Egypt (Ex 5:4–19; Deut 26:6), but did not practice it until after the institution of the monarchy (1 Sam 8:12, 16–17). David imposed it on the Ammonites (2 Sam 12:31). Solomon developed it to the full in undertaking a colossal building programme – the temple, the palace, the fortification of Jerusalem and the garrison towns (1 Kings 9:15–19). The labour force was made up partly of Canaanites (1 Kings 9:20–22), who were reduced to the position of abject slavery (similar to that of the Hebrews in Egypt), but also of Israelites (1 Kings 5:13), though their situation was somewhat more tolerable than complete slavery (1 Kings 9:22). However, the forced labour levy was seen as an intolerable burden by the people. It incited Jeroboam to revolt (1 Kings 11:26f), and is given as the main reason for the political division after Solomon (1 Kings 12:4–16). It is interesting to note that much later Jeremiah castigates Jehoiachim for building his palace by forced labour, refusing to pay the workers any wages. He denounces this practice as 'The shedding of innocent blood' and 'practising oppression and violence' (Jer 22:13–17). At the time of Nehemiah, in contrast, the walls of Jerusalem were rebuilt by teams of volunteers (Neh 2:17–18).

Finally, we may note some of the economic consequences of monarchy. It brought with it the practice of feifs – land and other privileges granted in exchange for military service or some other form of personal loyalty to the king. This was an early example of feudalism.

Though this practice was widespread in the ancient Near East when Israel first appeared as a people, it was unknown among the Hebrews till the rise of monarchy. Because it encouraged the personal accumulation of wealth, it effectively broke the early ideal of equality between tribes and households.

Riches were accumulated in this period not only through the expansion of immovable property (land and houses – cf Is 5:8), but also through the growth of commerce. In an earlier period, the producer sold direct to the consumer, avoiding the need for a middle man. The producer was both wholesaler and retailer. Later (most likely in Solomon's reign) commerce arose as an occupation and a merchant class was born.

With the centralising of power and force in Israel, there was no restraint on the selfish, greedy and exploitative accumulation of wealth by a few in the nation. However, the leaders were never allowed to forget the terms under which they were constituted a people whom God protected. Even in a passage reckoned to be favourable to the institution of monarchy (Deut 17:14–17), there are severe warnings against accumulating riches for personal gratification:

> You may indeed set as king over you him whom the Lord your God will choose.... Only he must not multiply horses for himself, or cause the people to return to Egypt in order to multiply horses.... You shall never return that way again.... *Nor shall he greatly multiply for himself silver and gold.*

A high military budget and the gaining of personal wealth are seen as a return to the conditions of Egypt, an effective turning back from the liberated life to which God called his people at Sinai.

As a counter-balance to the political power of the king and his court, God raised up prophets – Samuel, Nathan, Abijah, Elijah, Elisha and the writing prophets (Isaiah and the rest). They were the nation's conscience, calling the leadership back to the terms of the covenant and warning it of the inevitable consequences of its policies. We now look at the message of one of those prophets.

2 Micah of Moresheth

We know little about the man except what we can glean from the prophecy. He is mentioned elsewhere only in the book of Jeremiah, as an example of a prophet to whom the king listened, in contrast to Jeremiah whom the king wanted to put to death (Jer 26:18).

His prophetic activities spanned three reigns: Jotham (740–732 BC), Ahaz (732–716) and Hezekiah (716–687) (Mic 1:1). He was a contemporary of Isaiah, Hosea and Amos – a formidable quartet!

Two outstanding political events took place during this period. Between 725 and 722 Samaria, the capital of the northern kingdom, was besieged and then captured by the Assyrian king, Sargon II. He deported some 27,000 captives to Damascus. This event was foretold in Micah 1:6–9. In 701 Sennacherib invaded the southern kingdom and threatened to take Jerusalem. He was defeated, however, as a result of Hezekiah heeding the prophetic message and repenting (Jer 26:16–19; Is 37). The king's military machine had nothing to do with victory. Micah also foretold this piece of history (Mic 1:12–15; 2:4; 5:5).

Micah lived at Moresheth-Gath in a region known as the Shephelah, just below the tableland of Judea, some twenty miles southwest of Jerusalem and about twenty miles west of Amos' birthplace of Tekoa. It was an exceptionally fertile region, because of the water that descended from the tableland. It is likely that he was a farmer with a small-holding (like thousands of other Hebrew families) (cf Mic 4:4). Moresheth was also situated half-way between Jerusalem and Gaza, near the fortress of Lachish, close to the Philistine cities of the plain and on the route taken by former invading armies. This would remind him of the havoc and destruction caused by Israel's enemies of former times and the threat of its repetition by the powerful Assyrian nation to the north.

He prophesied mainly in Jerusalem, directing his message against the political and religious leaders and the wealthy land-owners who lived in the capital.

(a) The situation of the nation

Micah's prophecy is divided between stern warnings about the state of the nation and a message of hope and comfort for all who turned to the Lord, doing what he required (Mic 6:8).

Micah's message represented what God thought of the political, economic and religious life of his people. It was a rebuke and a warning about specific incidents happening every day among the people.

(i) Corrupt politics (Mic 3:1–4, 9–11) Micah speaks directly to the public officials in Jerusalem. They are called 'heads of Jacob' and 'rulers of the house of Israel' to remind them

of their responsibility as leaders of a people whom God is particularly concerned about. In particular, they are the people responsible for administrating the law (Deut 16:18–20; 2 Chron 19:4–11).

They are supposed to be well acquainted with the process of sound law. The premise for a legal system to work is that the judges are wholly impartial and free from pressures to pervert justice. Instead, they despised justice, by distorting the difference between good and evil, and making violence into a way of life. Wrongdoing had become a deliberate and systematic part of public policy and life. The reason for exercising public office was financial gain.

The prophet uses powerful imagery from oriental cooking practices to describe the reality of violent oppression. Instead of receiving a just outcome to their complaints, the people are plunged into further suffering.

Yet these leaders will not live at peace with themselves. At some time in the future, circumstances will force them to cry out in anguish. The suffering they have brought on others will rebound on themselves. Their security will be shattered and their lives of selfish luxury will be brought to an abrupt end. Their cry to the Lord, however, is not like that of the poor, whose suffering is afflicted by others. They do not mean to change their lifestyle fundamentally. Therefore, the Lord will hide his face from them (cf Mic 4:9: 1 Sam 8:18; Is 1:15; Jer 11:11).

(ii) Economic exploitation (Mic 2:1–4) Micah is speaking about a situation of deliberate deception, viciousness and inhumanity. Groups of powerful people in the capital are devising ways and means of seizing the property and houses of small landowners (like the prophet). Their crime is a blatant contravening of the covenant Law, taking away from defenceless people their inheritance from the past.

For those who lost their property, the result involved more than simple economic impoverishment. In Israel's social order a man's identity and status rested on his household or family, dwelling-place and land . . . Lose (his inheritance), and he lost all the rights which were based on its possession; he had no 'place' in the community and had left only the life of a wage-labourer or a slave . . . The independence which came to him with his inheritance was gone. The plight of the weaker citizens in Israel and Judah, referred to so often by the eighth century prophets, was the result of an economic development which, supported by the policies of the royal court, had reached its climax in the eighth century. The rich and ruling classes were assembling estates in the country by skilfully managed loans and corrupt courts. The old family properties around the villages must have known through bitter experience the anguish and humiliation of this economic progress.[1]

Just as the evil leaders plan their enrichment, so God plans their ruin (Mic 2:3). They cannot ultimately expect to escape from their total disregard for God's laws and the people's rights. The punishment which God devises fits the crime: they will lose both their inheritance and all the property which they have illegally expropriated for themselves (Mic 2:4). Even in the future their inheritance will not be returned to them (Mic 2:5). Thinking they could gain for themselves more than justice allowed, they lose more than they originally set out with.

(iii) The manipulation of religion (Mic 2:6,11; 3:5,11; 5:12–14; 6:16) The corrupt, exploitative nature of life among the political leaders and rich landowners was matched by a religion trimmed to suit their tastes and justify what they were doing. Any qualms of conscience could be stifled by a swift sacrifice or two (Mic 6:6–7).

The direction of national religious life was in the hands of the priests and prophets. It is the latter who come in for the greatest condemnation. The former, mentioned only in Micah 3:11 ('her priests teach for a price'), had commercialised the worship of God and the interpretation of his law. Those who could afford it received from them a religious sanction to confirm them in their violent and corrupt practices (cf Mic 2:11).

The false prophets were in many ways more dangerous, for they sought to neutralise the authority of the true prophets' message. It is interesting to contrast the word often on their lips – *peace* (Mic 3:5) – with Micah's first word – *justice* (Mic 3:1). In the context this difference pinpoints the yawning gap between a true and false word from God.

The essence of their message was that they would be delivered as a nation from any serious misfortune (Mic 2:6; 3:11), that God is not particularly displeased with his people and that, therefore, he will not bring any serious harm upon them.

The kind of God which the false prophets portray is one who is indifferent to good and evil, and who, because he has bound himself to them by his covenant, will never bring judgement on his people. Theirs is a light-hearted, shallow view of God. Their view of religion is that it can be manipulated in the interests of those who control power (Mic 3:11). They display the typical arrogance of leaders with unchallenged power who refuse to acknowledge that their choice of injustice will lead to their own downfall and catastrophe for others (Mic 3:12).

If the true covenant faith in God becomes too uncomfortable, there are other, less demanding religions to hand (Mic 5:13–14; 6:16). Indeed, their view of the deity is thoroughly pagan: God is amoral and can be induced to prosper a people, whatever their ethical conduct.

> The 'nouveau riche' in Jerusalem had drawn prophet and priest into their own environment where money talked louder than God . . . These prophets were promising well-being in the name of God to those who paid them well, and so made shalom (peace) a matter of a transaction between patron and professional.[2]

(b) The promise of a new future

The other side of God's unalterable hostility to arrogant and unscrupulous power is the hope of a society of genuine peace and prosperity for all. This takes two forms in the book. Firstly, the prophet announces the birth of a wholly righteous ruler who will care for, and not exploit, the people (Mic 5:2ff). Secondly, he announces the coming of a new world order which speaks of the end of violence and a return to the ideal of full economic equality (Mic 4:1–4).

(i) The Shepherd Ruler (Mic 5:1–5) The warning of punishment came true. Jerusalem was under siege. Judah's darkest hour had come. The much-vaunted rulers were powerless to save the nation from calamity. The king the people had asked for centuries earlier failed to stem the tide of invading hordes. God mocks them – 'now why do you cry aloud? Is there no king in you? Has your counsellor perished that pangs have siezed you like a woman in labour?' (Mic 4:9). But, in stark contrast to the desolation and humiliation of the moment, a message of hope and encouragement is given.

A baby is to be born in David's city (cf Is 7:14; 9:6). He will be Israel's future ruler. Like David, he comes from a humble background (1 Sam 16:11, cf Judg 6:16; 1 Sam 9:21). Like David and Saul, he is not part of an already ruling dynasty, but is chosen directly by God to lead. He is not called king (*melek*), but ruler (*mosel*). This is perhaps to emphasise God's sole kingship or, perhaps, to avoid a term that had become debased. He is one of the people he has come to lead (cf Deut 17:15; Heb 2:11,17).

His leadership is described in terms of a shepherd (Mic 5:4, cf Mic 7:14) to emphasise guidance, protection and provision for the people's needs. His power, derived exclusively from God, will provide security and stability. As his sphere of rule will be universal, there will be no external threats. This messianic prophecy echoes many others (cf Ps 72:5; 2:8; 2 Sam 7:10; Zech 9:10; Ezek 34:23–24; 37:24–31).

(ii) Prosperity and security for all (Mic 4:1–4) The vision of a restored community stands in bold antithesis to the savage picture of havoc recorded in the previous verse (Mic 3:12). God himself will reconstruct society out of the devastation left by a policy of systematic corruption, injustice, violence and idolatry. People from all over the world will travel then

to Jerusalem, attracted by the transformation of its life based on keeping God's Law.

A contrast seems to be intended with Solomon's kingdom. In those days people also travelled from distant parts to consult Solomon, because the fame of his wisdom had spread far and wide (1 Kings 10:24). Nevertheless, he broke God's Law in numerous ways (by amassing wealth and arms for himself and living with women of other nations and religions) and died a disillusioned man (Eccles chapters 1–2). But in the future people will travel once again to Jerusalem to learn how to live by God's Law and enjoy the consequences of being part of God's rule.

The contrast with Solomon is continued in the utopian picture which displays the end of all violence and economic exploitation (Mic 3:3–4). Whereas Solomon's judgements had no bearing on the continuance of violence between nations, God's decisions (Mic 4:3) will mean the end of warfare. People will no longer need to settle disputes by resorting to arms. Not only that, but the resources which go into manufacturing weapons of destruction will be used for agricultural purposes.

The writer of the history of Solomon's reign comments that 'Judah and Israel dwelt in safety, from Dan even to Beer-sheba, every man under his vine and under his fig tree, all the days of Solomon' (1 Kings 4:25). Their security, however, was guaranteed by increasing the military power of the State, as the next verse goes on to say: 'Solomon also had forty thousand stalls of horses for his chariots and twelve thousand horsemen' (1 Kings 4:26; cf 2 Kings 18:31). However, in the case of Micah's prophecy, security is guaranteed by total disarmament – 'none shall make them afraid'.

The scene used to evoke the quality of peace . . . is . . . the ideal of the peasant farmer freed from the demands and threats of the military state . . . This picture of what will happen when . . . the nations make pilgrimage for the sake of *torah* (law) is restrained and inviting. The result is not a religious empire or a world subject in humiliation to a triumphant Israel. The nations bring their crises to YHWH (the Lord), their disputes are dealt with, and they depart. They are not dominated and incorporated in a power structure, but helped and led to a new policy that makes for life. The vision is not of some final stage of the struggle for power, but of its end, because nations come to see the real answer to their need in the word of YHWH.[3]

(3) Justice

As we have seen from a study of Micah, justice (*mishpat* and *sedeqah*) is a vitally important ingredient in the use of power by political leaders. It is much spoken about today, though not always with a great deal of clarity. The word occurs frequently in the Old Testament. Here I will elaborate briefly the five main components to justice which I mentioned on pages 86f.

(a) The impartial upholding of the Law

'Endow the king with your justice, O God, . . . He will judge your people in righteousness' (Ps 72:1–2). There are a number of different aspects to justice in this sense:

(i)   The impartial administration of the Law must be seen to be done (Deut 16:2);

(ii)   Justice is perverted by those who make decisions under the duress of either bribes or threats (Deut 16:19). So, the emphasis on exact weights and measures is a presupposition of justice (Deut 25:13–16);

(iii)   Justice must be available to the whole population, not only to one favoured section (Ex 18:13–26);

(iv)   Justice must not be delayed;

(v)   Justice is done when those who have done right are vindicated and those who have done evil punished (Lev 19:15; Prov 21:15);

(vi)   It is essential to the stability of a nation. Its absence brings a breakdown in harmony and leads to chaos (Prov 29:4).

(b) The right use of power

Justice is required because God looks for it and holds people accountable to exercise it (Is 5:7; 61:8). People in authority bear a particularly heavy responsibility to exhibit a life of uprightness and to maintain justice (1 Kings 10:9; Jer 22.1–5; Ezek Chapter 34).

The king in Israel, unlike other nations, was not vested with absolute and unchallengeable authority. He was not allowed to be a despot, for he was bound by God's covenant with the whole nation – a covenant which legislated on the basis of respect for life, dignity and the integrity of possessions for each family in the nation. The story of Saul reminds us that the Bible does not accept the idea of a divine right of kings.

Power and authority invested in an office should be used to establish an environment of truthfulness and rectitude in the nation. Their exercise can bring either a blessing or a curse upon a nation (Jer 7:5). God carefully watched the leaders of all nations, and is swift to judge those who pervert goodness (Ps 96:13).

(c) Defending the cause of the poor

According to the Bible, poverty may be due to one of three factors: misfortune, indolence or violent oppression. In the first and last case God's people are to vindicate those who suffer by meeting their material needs and by protecting them against exploitation (Ps 72.4).

Defending the cause of the defenceless is a necessary response to God's action in delivering his people from oppression in Egypt (Ex 23:9). It means standing alongside them when everyone else has abandoned them to their fate (Eccles 4:1), being their advocate and deliverer (Prov 31:8–9).

The poor are to be defended against *fraud* (unjust balances), *exploitation* (unjust wages) and *oppression* (the unjust loss of goods). One might call this reverse discrimination, giving partiality to those with no protection in society. The rabbis used to say that in a law court an orphan's case should be heard first, then that of a widow, then a woman before a man. In civil suits widows and orphans were to receive the benefit of the doubt (cf Deut 10:18; 27:19). The defence of the poor is at the very heart of God's justice – 'the Lord remains . . . faithful for ever. He upholds the cause of the oppressed and gives food to the hungry' (Ps 146:6–7).

(d) A life of complete integrity

God requires a personal life of active justice. We are to pursue a way of total honesty, which means renouncing all untruth, hypocrisy and duplicity. Our word is to be our bond. There should be no pretence, no giving of false witness, no misrepresentation of others nor distortion of what they say, and no evasion or exaggeration (Ex 20:16; 23:1; Deut 16:15–19; Ps 15:2–4; 24:4; 101:7; Prov 6:16–19; Is 28:17; Zeph 3:13; Ps 51:6).

(e) The salvation of the unrighteous

God not only requires justice in society (*justitia civilis*), he also enables people to be just (*justitia evangelica*). This latter notion, which is at the heart of the message about Jesus Christ, is not elaborated in the Old Testament. However, there is a hint of it in Isaiah 45:21. When God declares himself to be 'a righteous God and a Saviour', he means that he is a righteous God and *therefore* a Saviour (also Is 45:8; 46:13).

God's justice not only upholds the absolute distinction between right and wrong, it also brings the good to pass. To be complete, God's justice has to find a way of solving the problem of our continuous failure to be just. Forgiveness and a new beginning are part of God's justice, foreshadowed in the yearly celebration of the Day of Atonement. The magnificent passage in Micah 7:18–20 which sets forth God's mercy, faithfulness and forgiveness is used in the final part of the service to commemorate the Day of Atonement.

Conclusion

Our short survey of an institution, a book and a theme has come to an end. How can we use the historical facts, their interpretation and the teaching of the Old Testament to shape our opinions about and direct our actions within the political jungle of our modern world? One way would be to draw out from the passages we have studied that which God approves and that which he condemns, and then identify the equivalent situations today. I will suggest a few examples to indicate how this process might be developed.

God is clearly very particular about how power is used. Its supreme task is to uphold impartially the rule of the Law as this has been laid down in the book of the covenant. The rule of the Law is not an abstract notion – it has a very clear content. It is principally concerned to protect the family and the economic rights of the most vulnerable members of society.

The rule of the Law cannot be bent and twisted to suit the desires of those who have authority in the nation. On the contrary, right is seen be be done when they are the first to submit to its provisions. The first task of government is to do justice (Mic 6:8), even if this provokes conflict with those trying to work the system for their own advantage. One of the main strands of justice is compassion for the really needy. It also includes a policy of mercy in inflicting punishment upon law-breakers.

A modern equivalent to the rule of justice according to the book of the covenant might be a charter of rights. Such a charter, if it was going to correspond to the fundamental principles of government in Israel, would have to set out not only human (and animal?) rights, but also duties and responsibilities. For leaders not only had to refrain from using their power to gain wealth for themselves, but also had to find ways of meeting the genuine needs of the people.

From the calling of prophets to be the moral conscience of the nation and a counter-balance to the centralised power of the royal court, we can deduce the principle of an institutionalised opposition. Indeed, in circumstances where power is exercised in an extremely brutal, authoritarian and arbitrary way, prophetic resistence is sometimes the only way in which change may eventually come.

We have in mind something different from the official opposition of political parties in democratic, multi-party states. The problem of this type of opposition is that the rival parties hope to exercise power themselves, and therefore are bound by vested interests in their pursuit of confrontation. The opposition we have in mind has to be devoid of any concern to gain political power. Indeed, like Amos, who was 'neither a prophet nor a prophet's son', the members would have to be reluctant protagonists.

Prophetic opposition of this kind will probably arise automatically in an open, pluralist society. Its effectiveness will depend upon the standing in society of the people concerned, and a general perception that they personally are not interested in the exercise of government. A government might also gain credibility by instituting a consultative council, representative of important sectors of the community, which would be invited to give critical and constructive opinions on important policy issues. Clearly such a body would be the antithesis of a party-political policy institute or think-tank.

Finally, God's evident displeasure at the amassing of armaments has important consequences for modern political life. Not unnaturally, such a policy is a drain on financial resources and distorts economic life, being one of the major burdens on government expenditure. The existence of a non-elected, elite corps responsible only to the head of government or to departmental ministers can easily distort the balance of power in a nation.

Notes

1   James Mays *Micah* (London, SCM Press, 1976), p 64.
2   Ibid, p 83.
3   Ibid, p 99.

VIII

Applying the New Testament

For a moment we must return to the question of how the two Testaments are to be compared. It is commonly argued, and with justification, that the relationship between God's people and the State changed fundamentally with the coming of Christ. The *ekklesia* (Church) in the Old Testament is the whole assembly of the Hebrew people called into a covenant relationship with God. This *ekklesia* was co-extensive with one ethnic group, and this group also formed a comprehensive social and political entity, with laws to regulate the entire life of the people.

In the New Testament the *ekklesia* becomes multi-ethnic, and ceases to be a political community. Indeed, it would be ludicrous to try to enforce within its ranks some of the Old Testament laws (e.g. punishments for criminal acts), for it is a new community scattered among the nations. It is true that at periods of its subsequent history the Church became almost co-terminous with the State. Being a citizen and belonging to the Church were considered one and the same thing. However, this is now generally judged to be a major misunderstanding of the nature of the Church, reconstituted in Christ. Membership is by baptism in water and the Spirit, not by natural birth. Being a disciple of Christ may mean having to renounce family and national ties.

Moreover, the Church is a pilgrim community called to move (like Abraham) towards the fulfilment of God's sovereign reign over all things. It has set its face, therefore, towards the future transformation of all things when Christ comes again. The future reality of a new heaven and a new earth is a constant point of reference for its life and witness. It is also a rebuke and a challenge to political power and policies which in an unredeemed world can never wholly measure up to the standards of life under God's rule.

The essential identity of Christians is found in the life to come (their citizenship is in heaven), whereas political activity has to concern itself with this present existence. For all these reasons, the early Church, once it had become disassociated from Judaism, existed as a community only on the edges of political life. The thrust of the teaching of the New Testament seems to be directed towards personal salvation and the exemplary life of God's people in the midst of an alien and hostile world.

And yet, there are substantial examples of how the early Christians grappled with the problem of relating their own faith to the world of political power in their time. Indeed, they found it an imperative necessity to tie in their new sense of identity as God's redeemed people of the new covenant with their obligations and relationship to the old State.

As with the Old Testament, I can only scratch the surface of the rich variety of material in the Gospels, Acts, Epistles and Revelation. So, I have chosen again one institution (the State), one passage (Jn Chapters 18–19) and one theme (freedom) as instances of how we might use the New Testament to throw light on our attitude today to the world of politics.

1 The State

Using the term 'State' in relationship to the historical situation covered by the New Testament may create confusion. Obviously, no entity existed equivalent to our post-industrial, welfare, national unit that we call the State. Rather, we are talking about different levels of political organisation, authority and control. In the New Testament we are dealing perhaps with three different examples. Firstly, the global power of the Roman Empire; secondly, the city-state of Greek political tradition; and thirdly the rather complex quasi-religious, quasi-political interaction between various strands of leadership in Israel – the vassal-king Herod, the members of the Sanhedrin and the powerful Sadducean party.

The State as an institution, therefore, was not an abstract body, but a practical, living exercise of power according to the policies and laws of the groups who had control. Jesus Christ and the early Church experienced the State not as a theory but as a living reality in the form of leaders, policies and persecution.

Perhaps for this reason the early Church developed no systematic theory of the State (until Augustine). The State is recognised as a valid institution, ordained by God himself (Rom 13:1). As such it has certain rights and responsibilities. It has the right to expect respect (Rom 13:7; 1 Pet 2:17), co-operation (Rom 13:2) and the paying of taxes (Rom 13:7; Mk 12:15–17). Moreover, Christians are exhorted to pray for all in leadership positions in society, that the latter may create the conditions for a society at peace (1 Tim 2:1–2). The main responsibility of government is to maintain in society an effective distinction between right and wrong (1 Pet 2:14), and to spend the revenue collected with wisdom and fairness. Little more is said than this by way of a general, positive statement about the State.

There are, however, hints as to its proper function and role in either overt or implied criticisms. Jesus was well aware, for example of the State's excessive violence. Pilate's slaughter of certain Galileans whilst they were involved in religious activities in the temple is one instance explicitly mentioned (Lk 13:1–2). This was probably a hasty over-reaction by a group of soldiers, afraid that the Galileans were using the occasion (probably the Passover) to plan a seditious revolt (what today we would call a terrorist attack).

Owing to the build-up of opposition to the Roman presence in Palestine, Jesus predicted far worse violence to come. He clearly did not agree with the political and theological assumptions on which this opposition rested. His one direct quote on the policy of the 'freedom fighters' declared that it was a self-defeating exercise: 'all who take the sword will perish by the sword' (Mt 26:52). He seemed to accept Rome's presence and its right to levy taxes from its forcibly subjugated peoples: 'give to Caesar what is Caesar's' (22:21).

Yet Jesus relativised the authority of the State. The citizen's responsibility to the governing power was circumscribed by his unconditional loyalty to God. In one likely interpretation of the dispute about paying taxes, Jesus' reply is much more profoundly subversive than might at first sight appear. In the context of Jesus' emphatic teaching that no-one can simultaneously 'serve both God and Money' (Lk 16:13), he is saying '*give back*' (or hand over) to Caesar what belongs to him – namely, the wealth (represented by the Roman coin) on which the State's power and violence was built. But at the same time we are to hand over to God what belongs to him – the entire created life of the world, which he has appointed human beings to administer justly and selflessly as stewards.

Of course, the whole situation was a put-up job to trap Jesus into committing himself to one of two political positions, both vehemently promoted by their respective protagonists. On the one side, the fanatical revolutionary party was aiming to create a utopian state of their own imagination (cf Acts 1:6). On the other side, the collaborationists, because they benefitted opportunistically from the actual way power operated, were militantly hostile to any change which threatened their privileges.

Jesus brilliantly side-stepped the political trap and laid down a principle of action valid in every situation. He told the Sadducees to give themselves over entirely to God's rule as it was exercised through him ('seek first the kingdom of God and its justice'). He told the guerilla dissidents not to waste their time trying to dislodge the occupying force. The moment to resist would come when Caesar made demands incompatible with commitment to God's righteous rule.

The time when the early Christians had seriously to review

their relationship to the State arrived when they were subjected to systematic persecution on account of their confession of Jesus, Messiah and Lord. This turn of events is reflected in the book of Revelation. Here, then, the State is viewed in terms of its willingness to persecute a tiny, minority religious community who posed no political threat to its continuing authority and influence.

Perhaps the cause of opposition to the Church was that it represented a strange and different set of beliefs. It was accused of disloyalty to religion, the State and family life. Christians were accused of praying for the downfall of civilisation (that which existed) and being atheists (for not acknowledging the cult to the Emperor). In Domitian's reign some 40,000 Christians were slain! It is not surprising, therefore, that John's vision on Patmos portrays the dark, sinister side of the State.

Revelation is a prophecy (Rev 1:3; 22:9,19). The prophecy reveals how the mystery of evil is at work in human political institutions and how God acts to control, overrule and finally end it. It also shows how nations, because of their failure to acknowledge the living God, are obliged constantly to reproduce the patterns of past folly. Once the basic choice not to recognise a moral reality to which one is absolutely accountable has been made, the political options are limited (Rev 22:11).

Revelation points to a powerful expression of State idolatry, whose source is the deception which Satan causes (Rev 12:9; 20:3, 10). Deception results in a creeping belief in myths and illusions about power, freedom, security and law and order. The deceit is undergirded and promoted by false prophets (Rev 16:13; 19:20). Deception and idolatry then interact, producing an increasing spiral of falsehood (Rev 19:20). True prophecy, on the other hand, exposes every kind of delusive hope and political deceit.

Bearing in mind the comment on the dispute about taxes for the emperor and personal experience of how societies operate, one should hardly be surprised that the idolatry of the State is closely related (in Revelation) to economic advantages. Only those with the mark of the beast, either on their forehead or right hand, can engage in business (Rev 13:17). The mark of the beast was the image of the emperor, either on the coinage (the number 666 may well refer to the inscription on the coin, *A KAI DOMET. SEB GE* – 'Domitian Augustus Caesar, Emperor of the Germans') or on the red seal which validated all business transactions. The context suggests that economic sanctions were practised against Christians for not recognising the State's supreme authority.

Much of the picture of the judgement on Rome (Rev Chapter 18) is couched in terms of its economic life. It is a vigorous and disturbing picture of a society totally dedicated to the service of Mammon. Trade was so arranged that wealth flowed from the provinces to the metropolis. Part of the idolatry of the 'harlot' was to offer material luxury in exchange for submission to the system (Rev 18:3).

The material affluence of the imperial system is judged for three reasons:

First, it produced a false sense of security (Rev 18:7). As G B Caird has commented, 'it had an unquestioning faith in its own inexhaustible resources, unaccompanied by any sense of a deeper lack'.[1]

Secondly, it was created on the back of slavery and the exploitation of labour (Rev 18:13);

Thirdly, it resulted in a life of debauchery and lack of restraint. Rome's cruelty was notorious.

There is much in Revelation which reminds us of the Old Testament prophets' 'oracles on the nations'. Rome has repeated the evils of other empires. It stands in a long line of powerful nations that used their might and authority to gratify their greed and control the destiny of others – Egypt, Assyria, Tyre, Sidon, Babylon, Greece. John's final word is that 'the great harlot corrupted the earth with her fornication' (Rev 19:2).

We might call the biblical writers' account of the rise and fall of empires a 'theology of the cycle of power'. They noted that injustice, dishonesty, corruption, repression and exploitation are inevitably self-destructive, and they attri-

130 God's Word for a Complex World

buted the ruin and extinction of such powers to God's judgement: 'Fallen! Fallen is Babylon the Great!' (Rev 18:2); 'Babylon the great city shall be thrown down with violence, and shall be found no more' (Rev 18:21); 'mighty is the Lord God who judges her' (Rev 18:8).

2 The trial and execution of Jesus of Nazareth (Jn 18–19)

John's account of the last two days before Jesus' execution comes across as a powerful drama, with the main characters constantly entering and leaving the stage. Jesus is confronted by, or rather confronts, two of the levels of political authority we mentioned earlier: the Jewish Sanhedrin and the Roman colonial power. Briefly the story goes like this:

Act 1	Scene 1 – Jesus is arrested in the garden across the Kidron valley.
	Scene 2 – He is taken to two senior members of the Sanhedrin, Caiaphas the high priest and Annas his father-in-law.
	Scene 3 – Peter denies any knowledge of Jesus.
Act 2	Scene 1 – Jesus is brought to the Roman governor Pilate. There is a discussion between him and the Jewish leaders about what to do with him.
	Scene 2 – Jesus and Pilate converse alone inside the governor's palace.
	Scene 3 – Outside the palace members of the Sanhedrin persuade Pilate to pass the death sentence on Jesus.
Act 3	Scene 1 – Jesus is crucified.
	Scene 2 – On the cross he awaits death.
	Scene 3 – Jesus is buried in a near-by garden.

I intend only to concentrate on a few incidents within one or two of these scenes, because of their relevance to involvement in politics. This principle of selection is not intended to suggest that the rest of the material is not important for other reasons. Nor are we seeking to lift the incidents out of their context, but to understand them within the total drama of the trial.

First, we need to defend the conviction that this passage is relevant to political life. Not a few commentators would say that Jesus was really crucified on a charge of blasphemy, though the final accusation that stuck seemed to be political – he ought to die, because he has made himself the Son of God (Jn 19:7: cf 5:18: 10:33; Lev 24:16). In other words, the criminal charge was that Jesus affirmed the Incarnation.

However, this was no crime in the Romans' books. As far as Pilate was concerned it was a matter of a religious quibble amongst a highly volatile subject people. As the Jews were not allowed to pass the death sentence (Jn 18:31), they had to present Jesus on a charge that would convince the Roman governor that he ought to die. The most likely option was treason and sedition (Jn 19:12; cf Lk 23:2). So the offensive claim was changed from 'Son of God' to 'king'.

Now, there is some validity in this argument. The Jews were extremely jealous for the Law and for the honour of the divine name – 'the Lord our God, the Lord is one' (Deut 6:5). Jesus certainly gave the impression of acting with God's own authority in an unparalleled way, throwing down the gauntlet to the supreme religious authorities in Judaism. However, a number of indications suggest that Jesus was seen as much more than a threat to the current interpretation of the Old Testament Law.

Firstly, the Sanhedrin expressed the fear that if Jesus was allowed to continue his public ministry, the Romans would put severe restraints on their activities (Jn 11:48); to which the high priest replied that Jesus must be eliminated in order that the religious and political life of the nation could continue (Jn 11:50). John repeats the incident in his account of the meeting between Jesus and Annas (Jn 18:14). In other words, Jesus' death happened so that the limited political privileges of the ruling group in Israel should not be further eroded.

Secondly, the Sanhedrin were clearly worried by the size of Jesus' following. They were perturbed not only by what he said (a dispute about doctrine), but by what he achieved in terms of drawing a large section of the population away from allegiance to the ruling authorities. Thus. Caiaphas questioned Jesus about his disciples before he brought up the subject of his teaching (Jn 18:19). Only a few days before, perhaps without fully realising what they were doing, a great crowd of people had hailed him as the Messiah (12:12–19). Now the Messiah in those days was popularly seen as a political liberator. The common people would have seen the entry into Jerusalem as a re-enactment of the welcome given 150 years previously to Judas Maccabeus when he came to the city as the victor over the then colonial power.

Thirdly, the two titles, 'Son of God' and 'king' are brought together in the person of the Messiah. This is explicit in the Psalm where God declares, 'I have installed my king on Zion, my holy hill' and 'You are my Son; today I have become your Father' (Ps 2:6–7, cf 2 Sam 7:12–16). So in those days it would have been difficult to avoid the strong political overtones of claiming to be God's Son.

There can be little doubt, therefore, that though the charge was false, Jesus was crucified (the way the Romans dealt with those they considered subversives) for being a political agitator opposed to Roman rule. This fact by itself, irrespective of the real reasons for Jesus' death, brings the heart of Christian belief into the centre of politics.

However, we still have to face the fact that the Crucifixion was a serious miscarriage of justice. Though Jesus was put to death for being some kind of political leader, he himself repudiated any design on normal political power – 'My kingdom is not of this world. If it were, my servants would fight to prevent my arrest by the Jews' (Jn 18:36). According to popular belief, the Messiah when he came would have never have allowed himself to be captured by Israel's enemies.

Jesus stated his own attitude to the direct or implied accusation of desiring political recognition with the enigmatic words, 'my kingdom is not of this world'. This saying should not to be understood to mean that Christ's kingdom was something totally separate from life in this world, either a wholly internal or else a future reality. The text cannot mean that. '*Of* this world' means 'arising *from* the way this world is structured and organised'.

In other words, Jesus' kingdom and therefore his messiahship were qualitatively different, in the way they worked, from the power exercised either by the Sanhedrin or by Pilate. Nevertheless, the power of the latter was held in trust directly from God – 'you would have no power over me if it were not given to you from above' (Jn 19:11). Therefore, they were accountable to him for its use.

Two other aspects of this drama are worth dwelling on for the sake of our present interests. Firstly, there is the way in which Pilate abused his authority. Probably, he was caught in the typical political dilemma between doing what was right and what was expedient. He was convinced that Jesus posed no real threat to the law and order he administered. Therefore, according to the law he had been sent to uphold, there was 'no basis for a charge against him' (Jn 18:38;). He knew that the dispute between the Sanhedrin and Jesus was over matters of a religion he did not understand, nor care about. At the same time, he wanted to minimise any possible disturbance at the Passover festival. With the great influx of Jews into the capital to celebrate the feast, it had become a notorious period of unrest.

To begin with he followed the path of legal justice. solemnly declaring Jesus innocent three times. But, in the face of the Sanhedrin's grim determination, he first temporised and finally gave in. Perhaps it was a justifiable fear that adverse reports would reach Rome (the Jews had already complained about his insensitive actions before) that finally persuaded him to go through with the blatant miscarriage of justice (Jn 19:12).

Secondly, there is the remarkable behaviour of the Jewish leaders. Pilate was largely unaware of the nature of the episode he was so reluctantly part of. He was confused, asking questions to which he received no answer that made sense to him. The real drama went on behind the scenes. In the final act it was the Jews rather than Jesus who were condemned out of their own mouth.

Jesus is accused of blasphemy, and therefore, according to the Law, deserves to die. However, in order to secure the death sentence against Jesus the same Jews are forced to make an incredibly blasphemous confession – 'we have no king but Caesar' (Jn 19:15). At one level what they said was true, for they had in practice abandoned the kingdom of God. However, it was not *the* truth, but a fundamental denial of their covenant relationship to God. In order to deny the truth about Jesus (cf Jn 18:37), they had to confess the final, great untruth about their faith. Beside this amazing statement, Jesus' supposed blasphemy pales into insignificance.

The drama of the Crucifixion underlines the pressure of political expediency. Jesus' real threat to the Jewish leaders was to challenge the religious base on which their political and economic power rested. Their interpretation of the Law excluded ordinary people from gaining access to the elite religious communities. This also meant that they were barred from participating in the civil community (Jn 7:49). Jesus, on the contrary, offered to all who accepted and followed him knowledge of the truth (including the truth about political power and its exercise), setting each of them free from the control of the self-appointed guardians of conventional wisdom and morality in society (8:31–32, 34–36, 40, 45–46). It is with a magnificent sense of the nature of the drama that, immediately after the Jewish leaders pervert the truth with blatant and apalling frankness, John places Pilate's decision to hand Jesus over to execution (Jn 19:16).

3 Freedom

The notion of freedom implies a situation where people are being confined or restrained. A bird is created to fly. It is free when there are no restrictions on its natural activity. Being put in a cage is, for a bird, the very opposite of freedom.

The New Testament has much to say about freedom for individuals and communities. It assumes that human beings are created for a certain kind of freedom, but that the path to that freedom is obstructed by a number of powerful constraints. In a number of important respects the biblical view of freedom contradicts the general view of freedom which has captured the imagination of the modern world.

Freedom is at the heart of the message of Jesus Christ. Christ came into the world to make people free (Gal 5:1; 2 Cor 3:17). In the New Testament view of human life, however, human beings are not automatically on the path to freedom, only needing a little religious push to attain their complete liberation. Indeed religion itself is an aspect of human life which hinders freedom. The New Testament insists that freedom is the result solely of liberation – 'he has sent me to proclaim release to the captives ... to set at liberty those who are oppressed' (Lk 4:18). Freedom through liberation implies that we are trapped in a situation in which hostile powers force us to obey them.

In the New Testament four fundamental realities of our human existence threaten and crush us: God's righteous anger, sin, the law and death. If we want to be human as God intends, we have to be freed from these realities. We will describe briefly the problem in each case.

(a) God's righteous anger (Rom 1:18; 5:9–11)

This is God's constant opposition to the way human beings pervert truth and goodness. It is manifested not as passive condemnation, but as active judgement. Those who choose (in their limited freedom) to exchange God's truth for their own version of the world are handed over to the consequences of their erroneous view of things: lust, passions, shameless acts of all kinds, conflict, violence and so on (Rom 1:26–32).

So what the unbeliever sees as a free choice in a pluralist society when it goes against God's perfect will for human life, the believer sees as the outworking of God's just judgement. Human beings are condemned to live out the inevitable consequences of their choosing to reject or ignore God. Their sphere of freedom, far from expanding, contracts in *ever-diminishing* circles. We talk of people being caught in a tangled web of their own making.

Being liberated from God's righteous anger means a life which lives out the truth about God and his world in *ever-increasing* circles of freedom.

(b) Sin (Rom 6:18–23)

There are many ways of describing sin. One central aspect of sin in the New Testament is that it is active unbelief. Faith is recognition of God, trust in his Word, faithfulness to his covenant and openness to receive his gift of grace. Unbelief is wilful ignorance of God, mistrust, unfaithfulness, rejection of the need for grace. It is self-sufficiency: the belief that all the resources needed for being a complete human being are contained in oneself and the environment.

Liberation from sin means being freed from a preoccupation with one's own righteousness and one's own right to be free.

(c) The Law (Rom 7)

Paul wrestled with the problem of the relation between the Law and the gospel. The Law expresses God's will: it is 'holy, just and good'. Nevertheless, on its own it aggravates the problem of sin.

(i) It makes insatiable desire quite explicit (Rom 7:7–8). It gives concrete names to our actions – adultery, murder, lying, greed, revenge – making sure that sin does not evaporate in a cloud of ambiguity and excuses.

(ii) It provokes a self-righteous spirit (Rom 2:23). This leads to pride and hypocrisy – I justify myself by comparing my good life with the 'greater' sins of others.

(iii) It opens up our insufficiency and impotence when conscience is aroused (Rom 8:3). The Law by itself produces a deep sense of guilt and self-accusation. It does not help us to see the way out. Moreover, trying to follow the Law can become an escape from fulfilling the requirements of mercy and justice. It often leads to scrupulosity – the attempt to follow the letter of the Law in every detail, pervaded by a fear of having forgotten some small item.

(d) Death (Rom 5:14, 17; 6:23; 7:9–11)

Death is not only the consequence of a life of sin, but also its actual experience – 'he who does not love, abides in death' (1 Jn 3:14); 'to set the mind on the flesh is death' (Rom 8:6). Perhaps one could say that death is the absence of the quality of life by which we become new human beings, recreated in Christ's image (Col 3:10; 2 Cor 4:16). Death is the choice of a way of life which substitutes our view of what it means to be human for God's intention for us. It is seen in dramatic form in drug-addiction, alcoholism, obsessive consumerism and the search for gratification, fame and fortune. Death is futility: the substitution of a quality of life for the quantity of things owned.

4 Liberated for freedom

Freedom from the dreadful realities of sin and its consequences comes through the sacrifice of Jesus Christ's death (Gal 3:13; 2 Cor 5:21; Gal 4:4–5). There is no other possible way. Freedom is not so much a possession as a new sphere of action, with new possibilities. Freedom is the result of being born into a new way of life (Tit 3:5–6) controlled by Christ's Spirit (Rom 8:9–11; Gal 5:16,25).

Those who believe that Jesus Christ has liberated them from God's righteous anger, unbelief, legalism and futility are free to be like Christ, who is the pattern of a restored, healed, whole human life. They are free to love and serve others, free to forgive and be forgiven, free to be people of hope and encouragement where there is doubt and despair, free to know God as *Abba* (Daddy). In brief, the death and resurrection of Jesus Christ has made us free to choose what is true, good and right and to attain the goal for which he has created us.

5 Conclusion

One of the most crucial questions for politicians concerns the frame of reference for their political activity and choices. What view of human life guides the goals they set for themselves? The real truth about human freedom is one of the most crucial issues which faces modern political life.

Probably the greatest aspiration of modern people is to be free. The quest for human rights is centred on the belief that human beings are by nature entitled to be free from restraints imposed by external forces. Of course, no-one imagines that any society can allow absolute liberty for self-expression. However, the right of individuals to shape their lives how they want, without outside interference, is a deeply and jealously guarded conviction.

Modern human beings have pursued freedom in two particular areas. First, freedom of choice in the market place. Controls on the individual's freedom to buy and sell is seen as a fundamental infringement of human rights. Economic freedom is regarded as both an expression and guarantee of political freedom, and therefore the most important safeguard of democracy. Secondly, freedom of belief and conscience. The notion of the primary and absolute right of personal choice has invaded our Western culture to such an extent that religious beliefs and moral values are now considered to be largely a private matter.

However, these two aspects of a modern society present serious contradictions to the practice of freedom. In the first case, the freedom claimed leads to the bondage of unfulfilled desire and false expectations. People are not satisfied by the restrictions which their limited buying power imposes. This leads to a scramble for resources. Freedom becomes relatively possible only for those able to survive and benefit by the resulting competition.

In the second case, the logical and political consequence of this kind of freedom is the fragmentation of society. The loss of a concensus about values and goals for society is a high price to pay for the freedom to follow whatever set of beliefs and norms we choose. No society can allow disunity to slide into anarchy. Society also abhors a vacuum where life seems aimless. As a result the group with the most coherent ideology will probably feel it has the duty to rescue society from chaos by imposing its views.

In my opinion, the debate over freedom is the key to understanding the dynamic of modern societies. However, much of the current understanding betrays a limited view. Freedom is seen almost entirely in terms of the absence of obstacles in the way of pursuing individual desires. These obstacles are seen as external, established authorities to which we are arbitrarily required to submit. We are unable to identify the constraints which are imposed on us either by the choices we make, or by the goals which the culture holds out to us as desirable.

Probably the greatest threat to human life in the world today does not come from the obvious suppression of individual and political freedoms in totalitarian societies, but from the superficial and one-sided understanding of freedom in the West. Dogged adherence to false beliefs and values has dulled the critical faculties of those who most strongly influence public opinion. That is why the New Testament insists that freedom is dependent on and flows as a consequence only of believing and doing the truth.

In political terms this means that government must know and abide by the true reason for its existence – to uphold and promote goodness and justice and restrain and punish wrongdoing as defined by God. It must be aware of and resist the temptation to convert itself or the policies it advocates into an independent entity, with a life of its own apart from the good of the people. The Roman Empire at the time of Domitian and the Sanhedrin at the time of Jesus are warning examples of what happens when political power becomes divorced from the truth about freedom.

Note

1   The Revelation of St. John the Divine, London, A & C Black, 1966, p 223.

IX

Explorations On The Move

---

1 Prayer, faith and reason

Discovering what is God's will for human life today by reading the Bible is a life-long process. There are no quick, easy answers. There are, however, indispensable aids which we can learn to use. Some, though absolutely fundamental, are difficult to describe in terms of a method which one can master. Prayer that the Spirit of God will give us deep insight into the mind of Christ and keep us from fanciful interpretations is one. Expecting God to show us the path to walk in is linked to our ability to pray, 'not my will, but yours be done.'

Understanding the Bible's meaning today assumes that we are seeking to remain in constant fellowship with the living God who caused the Bible to be written. The text cannot be treated as if it were like any other human piece of literature of the same period. Only as we try to live by the divine message contained in its pages will we fully understand what it is saying. Every attempt to interpret and apply the Bible is a pilgrimage in discipleship. It is done on the road as we follow the one who said, 'if you hold to my teaching, you are really my disciples. Then you will know the truth, and the truth will set you free' (Jn 8:31–32).

One of the major mistakes of modern biblical scholarship is the failure to combine adequately the intricate intellectual work of historical, textual and grammatical investigation with a life of personal spiritual growth in the fellowship of God's people. Scholarly pursuits do not take place in a spiritual vacuum. Correct exegesis is not an exercise which may be undertaken prior to commitment to be witnesses to Jesus Christ in word and deed. To appreciate fully the significance of the New Testament writings one must have a missionary heart. Luke, John, Paul, Peter and the rest were writing from within a community committed to the truth that the Good News of Jesus and the kingdom was the only hope for the transformation of the world. They understood that the meaning of Jesus Christ could only be grasped fully by those committed to sharing the gospel with others.

So, prayer and openness to follow Jesus Christ wherever he may lead us are conditions for hearing the Bible's message correctly. In many ways it would be better not to study the text unless one is prepared at every stage to allow one's way of life and the assumptions on which it is based to be challenged. Christ's rebuke to the Pharisees, 'Are you not in error because you do not know the Scriptures or the power of God?' (Mk 12:24) is not intended to suggest that they were ignorant of the content of the Bible. They had an extremely exact knowledge of God's commandments. They were rigorous in their search for the meaning and application of the text. Rather, Jesus accuses them of a distorted view of God. They were able to interpret Scripture so as to evade God's total demand on their lives – 'go and learn what this means: "I desire mercy, not sacrifice" ' (Mt 9:13).

No amount of technique, then, can provide the right framework in which to explore the Bible's significance today. The interpreter must at all times pray that God will give him or her a longing and hunger to do his will, in order to be in the right frame of mind to find out what the text really means (Jn 7:17). However, as we have stressed throughout, techniques cannot be by-passed. The right response to a wrong kind of intellectualism is not to abandon reason, but to use it correctly. It has to be placed in its proper context. Reason is not free in some theoretical way to follow the paths of investigation wherever they may lead. For one thing, it has, like every other aspect of human existence, been corrupted by sin. Freedom, therefore, is as likely to lead us away from truth as towards it; on balance, more likely to. For another thing, reason needs to be subject to the mind of God. It is quite impossible to separate the process of reasoning from belief. Unbelief does not exist, only true or false belief. Reason is free to accomplish its task only when allied to true belief. There is no state of limbo where it may operate independently.

The wisdom literature of the Old Testament gives us an important model for discovering the will of God. It is made up largely of rational thinking about careful observation of the world. Reason operates within the framework of a conviction that the universe belongs to God, who has shown us how to conduct our lives: 'here is the conclusion of the matter: fear God and keep his commandments, for this is the whole duty of man' (Eccles 12:13). Within this framework the human mind has great liberty to reflect creatively.

Before drawing out some conclusions from our study, I will attempt to show, by using a case study, how the different parts of the task of interpretation come together: the desire to do God's will, the place of reason and the use of the tools of the trade.

2 The use of wealth in society

At the beginning of this particular exercise I should make explicit two basic assumptions. Firstly, the Bible does not speak directly of any economic system. To use the parable of the talents as a reason for defending capitalism, or the Jerusalem Church's practice of all things in common as proof of the socialist ideal is to abuse the Bible. Both arguments fall into the trap of using isolated texts and making them say too much. As can be seen, when applied in this way they cancel each other out. A little knowledge can be a dangerous thing.

The Bible does, however, speak extensively and cogently of economic life, but at a different level of development from ours. There is a considerable historical gap. The Bible is concerned particularly about the effect of economic activity on human relationships, in the light of the reality of sin, of God's demands for justice and compassion and the promise of salvation by grace alone. This is the main perspective from which to discern the meaning of those texts which speak about the use of wealth.

Secondly, to decide on the merits of any contemporary economic process, we need to begin with an analysis of the present situation. Theory is important but, in the light of the Bible's insistence on the practical outcome of belief or unbelief, what actually happens on the ground is more important. It is of no earthly use to spin marvellous theories of what ought to be the case, if in practice it is clearly not working that way. Any theory to be adequate must be able to give reasons why alternative theories do not explain real life. In this sense true Christian thought is undoubtedly a critical reflection on the world as it is in the light of God's Word. The latter, of course, is also concerned about what the world might become.

(a) The first step is to define the crucial issues

I would suggest that we need to address three important questions: How is wealth created? For what purpose? And who should own it?

(i) The creation of wealth. Defining the meaning of wealth is a hazardous business. It is easy to beg many questions. However, we must know roughly what we are talking about. Hence, I understand wealth to be the total stock of possessions owned individually or corporately whose ownership can be exchanged for money or other goods. We are talking here of tangible assets such as land, houses, bank accounts, investments, industrial stock, premises and so on. Other forms of potential wealth-creation like human skills, training, professional connections and goodwill, though part of the process, are difficult to quantify.

Wealth is created through the production process. This has four contributory parts: raw materials (land and minerals), labour (agricultural, mining or manufacturing), capital (the reinvestment of past accumulated wealth) and technological advance. There is a basic difference of opinion amongst economists as to which of these four elements actually adds value to the original resources. Some work with what is called 'the labour theory of value': profit or wealth is the difference between the net output of an industry and the amount the worker is paid in wages. Or, to put it another way round, 'net output is the value added by labour to the constant capital.'[1] In other words, of the four factors of production, only the worker puts into the process more than he receives back in wages. All the others are either given (raw materials) or pay for themselves.

Others want to relate the value of goods and services both to the cost of producing them and to the peoples' demand for them in comparison to their general availability. Hence, for example, production is dependent on the investment of capital, and because capital represents the sacrifice involved in foregoing consumption by saving, it is part of the total cost. That is why capital should also be paid a wage or dividend.

The difference between these two views (generally between socialism and capitalism) is that for the latter capital as well as labour creates wealth, whilst for the former profits are a levy on the wealth which labour alone creates. Does the Bible in any way help us to resolve these divergent opinions?

(ii) The purpose of wealth-creation. When we ask questions about the purpose of economic life we move beyond those areas of life where economics as a discipline is the most appropriate tool to provide answers. We are touching the realm of values which human beings place on life. Values undoubtedly flow from a conscious or unconscious understanding of our existence. What do we consider to be the most important aspects of life? Why do we set ourselves particular goals?

Depending therefore on how we view life, we might give a variety of different answers to the question, Why create wealth? They are not necessarily contradictory, though there may be a fierce debate about priorities. Some will say that wealth is created to express our creative impulses. Others will emphasise the need to create paid work. Yet others will maintain that it responds to an innate human drive to gain power and influence others. Following some kind of utilitarian theory, another group may stress that the possession and consumption of goods and services maximises happiness. Finally, some will point to the goal of equality through sharing: wealth-creation is designed to meet everyone's basic needs for a dignified life – housing, clothing, a healthy diet, education and medical attention.

Does the Bible relate to these questions at all? Clearly it does, for its message has many things to say about the purpose and goals of human life. In fact it gives clearer answers to the question of the purpose of wealth than to its creation, for the latter is posed in terms strange to the experience of biblical communities. Nevertheless, questions of purpose are linked to those of wealth-creation, and both to the third main issue.

(iii) The ownership of wealth. The socialist view of ownership assumes the labour theory of value. The workers because they create wealth, should also own it. This might happen in one of two ways. In a cooperative system all the workers would own the shares and assets of the business, company or industry. Managers would then be accountable to the workforce, rather than to anonymous shareholders. In a totally socialist economy the government would hold all accumulated wealth in trust for the benefit of the whole community. This system assumes that the government is representative of the working class and always acts in their best interests.

The capitalist view of ownership assumes the more diffuse view of wealth-creation. All those who contribute to wealth-creation, whether workers or private or corporate lenders of finance, should have a stake in the ownership of the manufacturing process. It assumes, of course, that the value added in the process of production is not expropriated from the workers' labour,[2] but is the result of a total process whereby the factors of production are brought together to create a net profit for the company. In this case ownership tends to be divorced from moral considerations and made into an absolute right.

Again one might expect the Bible to say something on this question. We should not expect it, however, to use the terms of reference supplied by modern economic custom.

(b) The second step is to identify the biblical material

(i) The question of ownership. The Bible refers this issue back to its understanding of God and human beings. Ownership is never treated as an absolute value, apart from a human being's relationship to God and to others. Nor, conversely, is there any prohibition of ownership treated as a theory in isolation from these relationships. Every principle begins with the fact of Creation and its major implication that human beings are accountable for all their acts and beliefs to a transcendent moral Creator (Ex 24:3–7; Deut 26:16–17).

This means that ownership is a matter of human beings' relationship to the God who made them. The only absolute owner is God. He owns Creation (Lev 25:23; Ex 19:5; 1 Chron 29:11), and he owns humankind (Deut 14:2; 26:18; Tit 2:14; Rev 1:6). All other ownership is derivative. From the fact of Creation we deduce that human beings are leaseholders, not freeholders. They are called to be wise managers of what belongs to another. *Ownership is more about responsibilities than rights.* We are to administrate wealth faithfully for our own genuine well-being, that of our neighbour and future generations yet unborn. Pure self-interest cannot be a right motive for economic life. It is no more permissible than adultery or false testimony. In the life of Israel ownership was communal, not individual.

There is a second principle, which follows from the perversity of human nature. The Fall brought with it the twin evils of fear (the lack of security) and the craving for power (the attempt to gain security for oneself). This has a bearing on ownership in that the struggle for security against the fear of losing everything (nakedness) often leads to dispossessing others of their legitimate ownership. It is in this context that we should understand the story of Naboth's vineyard (1 Kings 21:1ff). God was not protecting any absolute right of private property. Rather, he was intent on protecting a relatively weak and vulnerable family from the greed and violence of a powerful king. We deduce from this story (as well as from the prohibition of theft and of removing the neighbour's landmark) that no-one has the right to use their superior power to take away what others need for life or what they produce for themselves.

This principle could be directed, in different ways, against both socialism and capitalism. Ownership was invested in the communal structure of the extended family, in order that this basic unit of society might be able to exercise responsible stewardship. The State has no right to deny this responsibility. At the same time, in order that everyone should have the same possibility of stewardship, the State has a right to intervene to check the unbalanced accumulation of wealth (this was the basic purpose of the Sabbatical and Jubilee regulations). The principle of responsible stewardship seems to point both to capitalist private ownership and socialist redistribution of wealth.

(ii) The creation and use of wealth I have argued elsewhere that the Bible helps to give us the right perspective on wealth by making a necessary distinction between human needs and wants.[3] Anything more than 'the bread we need for each day' is liable to spring from and result in greed. Paul calls this idolatry (Eph 5:5; Col 3:5), because it aims at both achieving security apart from God and making the satisfaction of pleasure into the highest goal of economic life.

The creation of wealth is good and right as long as the first priority of every human community is to satisfy the needs of all. This claim is prior to anyone's right to own and enjoy whatever they can pay for.

(c) The third step is to draw the right conclusions

By way of example I will suggest three conclusions that follow from this study. I have no wish to imply that other conclusions (though not contradictory ones) would not be equally valid.

(i) Economic life is not exempt from the critique of God's Word The creation and use of wealth is for the sake of human community life in God's world. Therefore, it is not free from moral values deriving from the meaning of human life. Because at the heart of creation are personal beings, there are no impersonal iron laws of economic development, independent of responsible human decision-making. The appeal to market forces or to the revolutionary struggle of the proletariat as reasons for not attending to the basic needs of people is an affront to the moral nature of human life as created by God.

At the same time, no one economic system may be deduced with certainty from the whole of the Bible. It speaks directly, but generally, about the creation, ownership and distribution of wealth. It also regards the systematic pursuit of possessions to be a false goal of life and therefore a denial of the true nature of human existence.

(ii) Both wealth-creation and distribution need protecting. If human beings were spontaneously unselfish, the use of wealth would not be a problem. Either capitalism or socialism would work perfectly to create wealth for the benefit of all. In a thoroughly imperfect world, however, some form of mixed economy seems the only way of dealing with the abuse of power, whether it is that of corporations, stock-markets, banking institutions, insurance agencies, pension funds, trade unions or the State. Political decisions relating to economic activity will depend both on what activities need stimulating and what imbalances need redressing.

(iii) The right to create wealth and the responsibility to share it If the main purpose of wealth-creation is to to satisfy the needs of every member of the community, then others have a claim on the fruit of my work (tangible possessions) and my talents (intangible possessions). There is my extended family, and there are my neighbours, especially those who are relatively unprotected from the harshness and uncertainty of commercial life – the widow, the orphan and the member

of a minority community. If others are prevented from working, then I have an obligation to share my excess, either by direct giving or through the local or national community.

From the entire argument concerning ownership we might conclude that the ideal from a biblical perspective in present circumstances is either the family ownership of small businesses or the workers' ownership of large industries. The raising of additional capital investment by the public sale of shares should not be linked to the ownership of companies. The integrity of share-ownership should be protected by reasonable returns on investment, not by the right to dictate policy to those daily operating the productive process. At the same time, vital national assets and raw materials should be publicly owned by a government genuinely accountable to the population for what it does with the wealth it owns on behalf of the entire community.

Conclusions

(a) What may we reasonably expect?

It will have become clear that the Bible cannot be used like a text-book, with an index at the back and straight answers to all questions in each chapter. It speaks God's Word to us, as it is allowed to be itself. The Bible is made up of many different stories within one basic story. The latter tells of two communities: one is a national entity, the people of Israel, descended from Abraham; the other is not a national unit, but a fellowship of people – Jews and Gentiles together – who accept that Jesus Christ is God's Son and the world's Saviour.

These two communities at different stages and in different ways have enjoyed a special relationship to God. He has spoken to them about himself and about themselves – who they are, what is the purpose of their existence and what he intends to do about the world in the future. The Bible is all about relationships: what they are intended to be, why they so easily become broken and how God restores them to perfection.

What we find, therefore, throughout the Bible are indications about how human beings should live together in community under the direction of God's revealed will, and what happens when they fail. Political decision-making in any field of human history should respond to the general and specific guidelines laid down in the two models of community the Bible gives us. Application of the model from one generation to another depends on being able to separate out the incidental and circumstantial elements from the central intent and purpose of each story.

(b) Is everything in interpretation relative?

Because of the need to transmit the message from one history and culture to another, the impression may be given that there are no fixed points for discovering God's will today. The diversity of modern cultures has led some Christians to come close to saying that what is applicable in one set of circumstances may be irrelevant in another. The common phrase, 'the world sets the agenda', seems often to mean in practice that the world also controls the Christian response.

It is vital, therefore, to stress that the God of the Bible is the only true God, who has clearly revealed himself as the Sovereign Lord of all peoples. He is neither a tribal deity, nor does he belong in some way only to the Christian faith.

Moreover, the Bible clearly states that, in spite of the diversity of peoples, who develop their own language, history and customs, there is a fundamental unity to human life. What is true at the level of our creation is repeated and deepened at the level of redemption – 'one body and one Spirit . . . one hope . . . one Lord, one faith, one baptism; one God and Father of all' (Eph 4:4–6). The models for life in community are based on God's character and the universal reality of human nature. These remain constant even when changing circumstances evoke different applications of the central facts of God's truth.

(c) Different ways of reading the Bible

Most Christians are, in general, exposed to the Bible on three occasions: the daily reading of texts with the aid of notes, group Bible study, and a weekly sermon. In each case the approach is likely to be devotional and chapter-by-chapter. This kind of study is admirable as long as it does not become a substitute for more systematic methods. Another important way of exploring the meaning of the biblical message is through thematic study. Tracing themes or words through the Bible helps to give us a vision of the unity of God's revelation.

This is the method behind my discussion earlier of justice. Any Christian can employ it by using a good cross-reference Bible, a concordance and biblical dictionaries. Other themes, of relevance to political life, which could be studied in this way, are power, authority, nation, citizenship, judgement, city, and so on.

We do need to be aware, however, of two major dangers in using this method: that of treating the whole Bible as of equal value, not recognizing that God's will is gradually unveiled (Rom 16:25–26), and that of not paying careful enough attention to the fuller context in which the word or theme is set.

(d) Making the discoveries for yourself

Throughout this book I have attempted to give concrete examples of how the Bible may be approached in order to discover God's will for us today. I finished with a more extended case-study on the use of wealth. The purpose has been to illustrate a method. I realise that the field of politics, as one instance of the art of biblical application, may not inspire everyone. Whatever aspect of the contemporary situation one wants to look at – marriage, family, education, medical science, the law, race relations, the use of violence to bring change, punishment, business practice, and so on – the overall method remains the same. One can, therefore, learn the trade by becoming an apprentice and actually practising the skills.

As we have chosen to use the political arena, another example we might explore is that of democracy. What are the right questions to ask? What is the relevant biblical material to hunt for? What conclusions should we draw for the present theory and practice of democracy?

Let me suggest a few leads that could be followed up. The ideal of democracy arose in the eighteenth century at the time when absolute hereditary power could no longer legitimate itself. It is expressed in the famous phrase of the American Declaration of Independence, 'government of the people by the people for the people'. But who are the people? At that time they did not apparently include women, native Indians or blacks. What are the conditions for genuinely representative government? What kind of power, remaining accountable to the whole population, is necessary for effective government? What dangers in the use of power need to be guarded against? How is the control of power most effectively achieved? Is the equality of all people self-evident? What is its theoretical basis? How is it to be expressed in society? How should change be brought about in a political system based on universal suffrage?

Some relevant material from the Bible might be: Jesus' attack on the oligarchic power of his day; the promise that rulers will be brought down from their thrones, that the humble will be lifted up and the meek will inherit the earth (Lk 1:52; Mt 5:5); the Church as a model for democracy; ancient Israel as the first form of power-sharing and a model for dispersed authority and leadership with consultation; the prophetic message of judgement on injustice and institutionalised violence as a withdrawal of legitimation from particular governments. As questions about actual democracies are probed and sharpened up, other passages and themes from the Bible may suggest themselves.

(e) Known by their fruits

Perhaps the test of faithfulness and integrity in interpretation and application which most accords with the Bible's way of thinking is that of the fruit produced. At least we need to ask seriously what happens as a result of reading the Bible. Does it seem to produce a legalistic stance, or libertarian conclusions? Are we confirmed in our withdrawal from society, or provoked to become involved? Does it make us more nationalistic or more universal in our appreciation of the rights of others? Does it weaken or strengthen our concern for evangelism and church-planting? Does it tend to produce beautiful intellectual schemes or deep practical compassion for a suffering and distraught humanity? Above all, do we become more mature people in fellowship with Jesus Christ, having the intellectual, spiritual and relational aspects of our life integrated under his direction? In the last resort, to correctly handle the word of truth (2 Tim 2:15) is for the sake of living by the truth (1 Jn 1:6).

Notes

1   Joan Robinson and John Eatwell, *An Introduction to Modern Economics* (Maidenhead, 1973) p 29
2   Profit-sharing schemes for employees, introduced by some companies, are perhaps a nod in the direction of admitting the labour theory of value.
3   Cf *A New World Coming* (Basingstoke, 1983) pp 68–74. This whole section also elaborates the distinction between the right of ownership and the illegitimacy of excessive accumulation.

For Further Reading

J. F. Balchin,	*Let the Bible Speak*. Leicester. 1981
R. Banks (ed.)	*Private Values and Public Policy: The Ethics of Decision-Making in Government Administration.* Canberra. 1983
O. R. Barclay (ed.)	*Pacifism and War*. Leicester. 1984
C. Bay	*Strategies of Political Emancipation*. Notre Dame. 1981
G. B. Caird	*The Language and Imagery of the Bible*. London. 1980
D. A. Carson (ed.)	*Biblical Inerpretation and the Church*. Exeter. 1984
B. Crick	*In Defence of Politics*. Harmondsworth. 1983
J. Dearlove and P. Saunders	*Introduction to British Politics: Analysing a Capitalist Democracy*. Cambridge. 1984
B. Goudzwaard	*Capitalism and Progress: A Diagnosis of Western Society*. Grand Rapids. 1979
B. Griffiths	*The Creation of Wealth*. London. 1984
J. Job (ed.)	*Studying God's Word*. Leicester. 1977
D. Levine	*Churches and Politics in Latin America*. Sage Publications, London
R. Longenecker	*Biblical Exegesis in the Apostolic Period*. Grand Rapids. 1975
J. R. Lucas	*Democracy and Participation*. Harmondsworth. 1976
R. Lundin, A. C. Thiselton, C. Walhout	*The Responsibility of Hermeneutics*. Exeter. 1985

I. H. Marshall   *New Testament Interpretation: Essays on Principles and Methods*. Exeter. 1979

P. Marshall   *Thine is the Kingdom: A Biblical Perspective on the Nature of Government and Politics Today*. Basingstoke. 1984

A. B. Mickelson   *Interpreting the Bible*. Grand Rapids. 1970

F. Milson   *Political Education: A Practical Guide for Christian Youth Workers*. Exeter. 1980

R. Mouw   *Politics and Biblical Drama*. Baker Books, USA

B. Nicholls (ed.)   *In Word and Deed: Evangelism and Social Responsibilities*. Exeter. 1985. (Chapters 3,4,6 and 8).

R. Padilla   'The Contextualisation of the Gospel' in *Mission Between the Times*. Grand Rapids. 1985

A. Pavadas   *The Indian Church in the Struggle for a New Society*. Bangalore. 1982

G. Ponton and P. Gill   *Introduction to Politics*. Oxford. 1984

R. C. Sproul   *Knowing God's Word*. London. 1980

J. R. W. Stott   *Issues Facing Christians Today*. Basingstoke. 1984

J. R. W. Stott   *Understanding the Bible*. Grand Rapids. 1982

J. R. W. Stott and R. Coote   *Down to Earth: Studies in Christianity and Culture*. Grand Rapids. 1980 (Chapters 5 and 6).

W. M. Swartley   *Slavery, Sabbath, War and Women: Case Issues in Biblical Interpretation*. Scottdale. 1983

H. F. Vos   *Effective Bible Study*. Grand Rapids. 1956

H. A. Virkler   *Hermeneutics: Principles and Processes of Biblical Interpretation*. Grand Rapids. 1981

P. Yoder   *From Word to Life: A Guide to the Art of Bible Study*. Scottdale. 1982

Biblical References

26.18	– 178
27.17	– 132
27.19	– 100,149

Joshua
24	– 126

Judges
6.16	– 145
7.22–23	– 136
8.22–23	– 103, 126
19–20	– 126

1 Samuel
8.5	– 104, 136
8.6–8	– 87
8.7	– 103
8.8	– 104, 105
8.12	– 137
8.12–13	– 104
8.14–15	– 104, 137
8.16–17	– 137
8.17	– 104
8.18	– 142
9.16	– 136
9.21	– 145
10.1–2	– 136
10.10	– 103
10.19	– 136
11.1ff.	– 136
11.15	– 136
12.2	– 136
12.11	– 136
14.52	– 134
16.11	– 145
17.25	– 137
22.2	– 134

2 Samuel
2.4	– 137
5.1–5	– 137
5.6ff.	– 137
5.21	– 137
7.10	– 146
7.12–16	– 162

8.1–14	– 137
8.18	– 137
11.1	– 137
12.31	– 138
15.18	– 137
20.7	– 137
21.15	– 137

1 Kings
4.24	– 146
4.25	– 147
4.26	– 147
5.13	– 138
9.15–19	– 138
9.19	– 137
9.20–22	– 138
10.9	– 148
10.24	– 146
11.14–25	– 137
12.4–16	– 138
21.1ff.	– 179
21.7	– 137
22.27	– 134

2 Kings
18.31	– 147

1 Chronicles
29.11	– 178

2 Chronicles
11.11–12	– 134
17.14	– 133
19.4–11	– 141
25.5	– 133

Nehemiah
2.17–18	– 138

Job
5.24	– 110
15.21	– 110

Psalms
2.6–7	– 162

Other Marshall Pickering Paperbacks

FORGIVE AND RESTORE

Don Baker

When a member of God's family, in this case a loved pastor, goes seriously off the rails in his personal life, the question looms large, 'What should the Church do about it?' 'Is it a matter for the church leadership only?' Should the wayward member be asked to leave or just relieved of responsibility? What should the congregation be told?

This book is a remarkable account of how one church dealt with such a highly charged and emotional crisis. It records in honest detail the ebb and flow of hope and despair, uncertainty and humanity, and relying throughout on biblical principles, it picks its way through a tangled mess to find a place of healing and restoration again.

WHEN YOU PRAY

Reginald East

Spiritual renewal has awakened in many Christians a deeper longing to know God more intimately. Prayer is the place where we personally meet God, yet it is often treated simply as the means for making requests for our needs, and offering our stilted, dutiful thanks. In this practical guide to prayer, Reginald East shows how we can establish a prayer relationship with God which is both spiritually and emotionally satisfying. Through understanding God and ourselves better, prayer can truly become an encounter with God, where we relax into Him, enjoy Him, listen as well as talk to Him and adventure into discovering His heart of love.

THE KINGDOM FACTOR

Roger Mitchell

We are living in extraordinary days. The rains of revival are on the way. The cloud is already bigger than a man's hand. All over the world is a resurgence of living Christianity. The coming in of the Kingdom of God in our generation is a real possibility. Whether or not this movement of God's spirit will finally bring the return of Jesus and the universal Kingdom of God will depend on the size of our vision of Jesus, the depth of our fellowship together in the Holy Spirit and the success of our evangelism. This can be the generation.

This is the thrust of evangelist Roger Mitchell's powerful book challenging Christians to bring in the Kingdom of God and to proclaim to a world desperately seeking answers that it is not some vague future hope, but a solid present.

MY FAITH

Compiler: Mary Elizabeth Callen

Well-known Christians invite us in through their private doors to reveal fascinating glimpses of their most personal thoughts and deepest convictions about their faith.

The late Laura Ashley and her husband frequently turned to the Bible for advice on her growing business. Botanist David Bellamy knows who to thank for all he enjoys in life. At 102, Catherine Bramwell-Booth still lives to spread the message of Christ. Lord (Len) Murray found God in the poverty of London's East End. The presence of Christ transformed the agony of torture into 'a privilege' for Dr Sheila Cassidy. For Anne Watson, God became more real and more mysterious during her husband David's illness and death.

Their moments of peace, doubt, anger and pure joy are common to us all, yet their experiences confirm the uniqueness of God's love for each individual.

If you wish to receive *regular information* about *new books,* please send your name and address to:

London Bible Warehouse
PO Box 123
Basingstoke
Hants RG23 7NL

Name...

Address...

....

....

....

I am especially interested in:
- [ ] Biographies
- [ ] Fiction
- [ ] Christian living
- [ ] Issue related books
- [ ] Academic books
- [ ] Bible study aids
- [ ] Children's books
- [ ] Music
- [ ] Other subjects